The Complete Book of
VEGETABLE GARDENING & CANNING

banner press, inc.

CONTENTS

GROWING VEGETABLES

Selecting a Site

A back yard or some other plot near your home in full sunlight is the most convenient spot for a home vegetable garden. However, poor drainage, shallow soil, and shade from buildings or trees may mean the garden must be located in an area farther from the house.

In planning your garden, consider what and how much you will plant. It is better to have a small garden well maintained than a large one neglected and full of weeds. Diagram the garden rows on paper and note the length you wish to assign to each vegetable. Use a scale of a selected number of feet to an inch. Then you can decide how much seed and how many plants to buy.

Consider also the possibility of working your vegetables in plots in front of your shrubbery. Many vegetables are ornamental in appearance. Some vegetables can be grown in your flower beds; others can be grown entirely in containers.

The amount of sunlight your garden gets must also be considered. Leafy vegetables, for example, can be grown in partial shade but vegetables producing fruit must be grown in direct sunlight.

Protecting the Garden

Usually, the garden should be surrounded by a fence sufficiently high and close-woven to keep out dogs, rabbits, and other animals. The damage done by stray animals during a season or two can equal the cost of a fence. A fence also can serve as a trellis for beans, peas, tomatoes, and other crops that need support.

In most sections of the country, rodents of various kinds damage garden crops. In the East, moles and mice cause much injury. Moles burrow under the plants, causing the soil to dry out around the roots. Mice either work independently or follow the burrows made by moles, destroying newly planted seeds and young plants. In the West, ground squirrels and prairie dogs damage vegetable gardens. Most of these pests can be partially controlled with traps.

Soil, Drainage, and Sunshine

Fertile, deep, friable, well-drained soil is necessary for a successful garden. The exact type of soil is not so important as that it be well drained, well supplied with organic matter, retentive of moisture, and reasonably free of stones. The kind of subsoil also is vitally important. Hard shale, rock ledges, gravel beds, very deep sand, or a hardpan under the surface soil is likely to make the development of high-grade garden soil extremely difficult or impossible. On the other hand, infertile soil that has good physical properties can be made pro-

1

ductive by using organic matter, lime, commercial fertilizer, and other soil improving materials.

Good drainage of the soil is essential. Soil drainage may often be improved by installing agricultural tile, digging ditches, and sometimes by plowing deep into the subsoil. The garden should be free of low places where water might stand after a heavy rain. Water from surrounding land should not drain into the garden, and there should be no danger of flooding by overflow from nearby streams.

Good air drainage is necessary to lessen the danger of damage by frost. A garden on a slope that has free movement of air to lower levels is most likely to escape late-spring and early-autumn frost damage.

A gentle slope of not more than 1½ percent facing in a southerly direction helps early crops get started. In sections that have strong winds, a windbreak of board fence, hedge, or trees on the windward side of the garden is recommended. Hedges and other living windbreaks should be far enough away from the garden to prevent shade or roots from interferring with the garden crops.

The garden should get the direct rays of the sun all day if possible. Some crops can tolerate partial shade, but no amount of fertilizer, water, or care can replace needed sunshine. Even where trees do not shade garden crops, tree roots may penetrate far into the soil and rob crops of moisture and plant food.

Damage to garden crops by tree roots may be largely prevented by digging a trench 1½ to 2 feet deep between the trees and the garden, cutting all the tree roots that cross the trench. Then put a barrier of waste sheet metal or heavy roofing paper along one wall of the trench and refill it. This usually prevents root damage for several years.

Preparing the Soil

Good soil for growing vegetables must be protected by proper cultivation, use of organic matter, maintenance of soil fertility, and control of plant pests. Properly prepared soil provides a desirable medium for root development, absorbs water and air rapidly, and usually does not crust badly.

Tillage practices do not automatically create good garden soil. Tillage is needed to control weeds, mix mulch or crop residues into the soil, and to alter soil structure. Unnecessary tillage increases crusting on the soil surface, and if the soil is wet, tillage compacts it.

Fertility requirements differ between long and short growing seasons and among soil types. In almost every State, the Extension Service will test soils and provide fertilizer recommendations.

Plant pests compete with garden crops and impair their growth. These pests include weeds, insects, fungi, bacteria, viruses, and nematodes. They must be controlled or the garden will not succeed. However, chemical controls must be used carefully to prevent damage to neighboring crops or subsequent crops. When mechanical and chemical controls do not work, crops that are resistant to the pests should be planted in the area for a season or two.

The time and method of preparing the garden for planting depend on the type of soil and the location. Heavy clay soils in the northern sections are frequently benefited by fall plowing and exposure to freezing and thawing during the winter, but when the garden is cover-cropped, it should not be plowed until early spring. In general, garden soils should be cover-cropped during the winter to control erosion and to add organic matter. Gardens in the dry-land areas should be plowed and left rough in the fall, so that the soil will absorb and retain moisture that falls during the winter. Sandy soils, as a rule, should be cover-cropped, then spring-plowed. Whenever there is a heavy sod or growth of cover crop, the land should be plowed well in advance of planting and the soil disked several times to aid in the decay and incorporation of the material. Land receiving applications of coarse manure either before or after plowing should have the same treatment.

Soils should not be plowed or worked while wet unless the work will certainly be followed by severe freezing weather. Sandy soils and

2

those containing high proportions of organic matter—peats and mucks for example—bear plowing and working at higher moisture content than do heavy clay soils. The usual test is to squeeze together a handful of soil. If it sticks together in a ball and does not readily crumble under slight pressure by the thumb and finger, it is too wet for plowing or working. When examining soil to determine if it is dry enough to work, samples should be taken both at and a few inches below the surface. The surface may be dry enough, but the lower layers too wet, for working. Soil that sticks to the plow or to other tools is usually too wet. A shiny, unbroken surface of the turned furrow is another indication of a dangerously wet soil condition.

Fall-plowed land should be left rough until spring, when it may be prepared by disking, harrowing, or other methods. Spring-plowed land should be worked into a suitable seedbed immediately after plowing. Seeds germinate and plants grow more readily on a reasonably fine, well-prepared soil than on a coarse, lumpy one, and thorough preparation greatly reduces the work of planting and caring for the crops. It is possible, however, to overdo the preparation of some heavy soils. They should be brought to a somewhat granular rather than a powdery-fine condition for planting. Spading instead of plowing is sometimes advisable in preparing small areas, such as beds for extra-early crops of lettuce, onions, beets, and carrots.

Organic Matter

Organic matter improves soil as a growing medium for plants. It helps release nitrogen, minerals, and other nutrients for plant use when it decays. A mulch of partially rotted straw, compost, or undecomposed crop residue on the soil helps keep the soil surface from crusting, retards water loss from the soil, and keeps weeds from growing.

Practically any plant material can be composted for use in the garden. Leaves, old sod, lawn clippings, straw, and plant refuse from the garden or kitchen can be used. Often, leaves can be obtained from neighbors who do not use them or from street sweepings.

The purpose of composting plant refuse or debris is to decay it so that it can be easily worked into the soil and will not be unsightly when used in the garden. Composting material should be kept moist and supplied with commercial fertilizer, particularly nitrogen, to make it decay faster and more thoroughly.

The usual practice in building a compost pile is to accumulate the organic material in some out-of-the-way place in the garden. It can be built on open ground or in a bin made of cinder blocks, rough boards, or wire fence. The sides of the bin should not be airtight or watertight. A convenient time to make a compost pile is in the fall when leaves are plentiful (fig. 1).

In building the compost pile, spread out a layer of plant refuse about 6 inches deep and add one-half pound or one cupful of 10-10-10, 10-20-10, or 10-6-4 fertilizer to each 10 square feet of surface. Then add 1 inch of soil and enough water to moisten but not to soak it. This process is repeated until the pile is 4 to 5 feet high. Make the top of the pile concave to catch rainwater.

If alkaline compost is wanted, ground limestone can be spread in the pile at the same rate as the fertilizer.

The compost pile will not decay rapidly until the weather warms up in spring and summer. In midsummer, decay can be hastened by forking over the pile so moisture can get to parts

Figure 1.—Making a new compost pile.

3

that have remained dry. The compost should be ready for use by the end of the first summer (fig. 2).

For a continuing supply of compost, a new pile should be built every year. Compost can be used as a mulch, or worked into flower beds and the vegetable garden. (fig. 3).

When properly prepared and thoroughly decayed, compost is not likely to harbor diseases or insects. If the compost is used in soil where an attempt is made to control plant diseases, or if it is mixed with soil used for raising seedlings, the soil should be disinfected with chemicals recommended by your county agricultural agent or State agricultural college.

Commercial Fertilizers

Commercial fertilizers may be used to advantage in most farm gardens, the composition and rate of application depending on locality, soil, and crops to be grown. On some soils with natural high fertility only nitrogen or compost may be needed. The use of fertilizers that also contain small amounts of copper, zinc, manganese, and other minor soil elements is necessary only in districts known to be deficient in those elements. State experiment station recommendations should be followed. Leafy crops, such as spinach, cabbage, kale, and lettuce, which often require more nitrogen than other garden crops, may be stimulated by side dress-

Figure 3.—Using a soil-compost mixture under and around plants in the garden.

ings. As a rule, the tuber and root crops, including potatoes, sweetpotatoes, beets, carrots, turnips, and parsnips, need a higher percentage of potash than other vegetables.

The quantity of fertilizer to use depends on the natural fertility of the soil, the amounts of organic matter and fertilizer used in recent years, and the crops being grown. Tomatoes and beans, for example, normally require only moderate amounts of fertilizer, especially nitrogen; whereas onions, celery, lettuce, the root crops, and potatoes respond profitably to relatively large applications. In some cases, 300 pounds of commercial fertilizer may be sufficient on a half-acre garden; in other cases, as much as 1,000 to 1,200 pounds can be used to advantage.

Commercial fertilizers, as a rule, should be applied either a few days before planting or when the crops are planted. A good practice is to plow the land, spread the fertilizer from a pail or with a fertilizer distributor, then harrow the soil two or three times to get it in proper condition and at the same time mix the fertilizer with it. If the soil is left extremely rough by the plow, it should be harrowed once, lightly, before fertilizing. For row crops, like potatoes and sweetpotatoes, the fertilizer may be scattered in the rows, taking care to mix it thoroughly with the soil before the seed is dropped, or, in the case of sweetpotatoes, before the ridges are thrown up.

Figure 2.—Compost ready for use in the garden.

Application of the fertilizer in furrows along each side of the row at planting time does away with the danger of injury to seeds and plants that is likely to follow direct application of the material under the row. The fertilizer should be placed so that it will lie 2 to 3 inches to one side of the seed and at about the same level as, or a little lower than, the seed.

The roots of most garden crops spread to considerable distances, reaching throughout the surface soil. Fertilizer applied to the entire area, therefore, will be reached by the plants, but not always to best advantage. Placing fertilizer too near seedlings or young plants is likely to cause burning of the roots. The fertilizer should be sown alongside the rows and cultivated into the topsoil, taking care to keep it off the leaves so far as practicable.

Heavy yields of top-quality vegetables cannot be obtained without an abundance of available plant food in the soil. However, failure to bear fruit and even injury to the plants may result from the use of too much plant nutrient, particularly chemical fertilizers, or from an unbalanced nutrient condition in the soil. Because of the small quantities of fertilizer required for short rows and small plots it is easy to apply too much fertilizer. The chemical fertilizers to be applied should always be weighed or measured. Table 1 shows how much fertilizer to apply to each 50 or 100 feet of garden row or to each 100 to 2,000 square feet of garden area.

TABLE 1.—*Approximate rates of fertilizer application per 50 or 100 feet of garden row, and per 100 to 2,000 square feet of garden area, corresponding to given rates per acre.*

Measurement	Weight of fertilizer to apply when the weight to be applied per acre is—			
	100 pounds	400 pounds	800 pounds	1,200 pounds
Space between rows, and row length (feet):	*Pounds*	*Pounds*	*Pounds*	*Pounds*
2 wide, 50 long _____	0.25	1.0	2.0	3.0
2 wide, 100 long _____	.50	2.0	4.0	6.0
2½ wide, 50 long _____	.30	1.2	2.4	3.6
2½ wide, 100 long _____	.60	2.4	4.8	7.2
3 wide, 50 long _____	.35	1.4	2.8	4.2
3 wide, 100 long _____	.70	2.8	5.6	8.4
Area (square feet):				
100 _____	.25	1.0	2.0	3.0
500 _____	1.25	5.0	10.0	15.0
1,000 _____	2.50	10.0	20.0	30.0
1,500 _____	3.75	15.0	30.0	45.0
2,000 _____	5.00	20.0	40.0	60.0

If it is more convenient to measure the material than to weigh it, pounds of common garden fertilizer, ammonium phosphate, or muriate of potash, may be converted roughly to pints or cups by allowing 1 pint, or 2 kitchen measuring cups, to a pound. For example, table 1 gives 0.25 pound for a 100-pound-per-acre application to 100 square feet. This would call for about ¼ pint, or ½ cup, of fertilizer. Ground limestone weighs about 1⅓ times as much as the same volume of water; therefore, measured quantities of this material should be about one-fourth less than those calculated as equivalent to the weights in the table. For example, ¾ pint of ground limestone weighs about 1 pound. Ammonium sulfate and granular ammonium nitrate are much lighter, weighing about seven-tenths as much as the same volumes of water; therefore, volumes of these substances calculated by the foregoing method should be increased by about one-third.

Liming

Lime, ground limestone, marl, or ground oyster-shells on garden soils serves a threefold purpose: (1) To supply calcium and other plant nutrients; (2) to reduce soil acidity; (3) to improve the physical character of certain heavy soils. As a rule, asparagus, celery, beets, spinach, and carrots are benefited by moderate applications of lime, especially on soils that are naturally deficient in calcium. Dolomitic limestone should be used on soils deficient in magnesium. Most garden vegetables do best on soils that are slightly acid and may be injured by the application of lime in excess of their requirements. For this reason lime should be applied only when tests show it to be necessary. In no case should the material be applied in larger quantities than the test indicates. Most garden soils that are in a high state of fertility do not require the addition of lime.

With good drainage, plenty of organic matter in the soil, and the moderate use of commercial fertilizers, the growth requirements of nearly all vegetables may be fully met. The local garden leader, county agent, or State experiment station can supply information on soil tests that can be made for each locality.

Lime, when needed, is spread after plowing and is well mixed with the topsoil by harrowing, disking, or cultivating. Burned lime or hydrated lime should not be applied at the same time as commercial fertilizers or mixed with them, because loss of nitrogen is likely to result, thus destroying part of the plant nutrient value. As a rule, lime should be applied in the spring, because some of it may be washed from the soil during winter. Any of the various forms of lime, such as hydrated and air-slacked lime, may be used but the unburned, finely ground, dolomitic limestone is best. Fifty-six pounds of burned lime or 74 pounds of hydrated lime is equivalent to 100 pounds of ground limestone. Finely ground oystershells and marl are frequently used as substitutes for limestone. Lime should not be used on land that is being planted to potatoes unless the soil is extremely acid, because very low soil acidity increases the development of potato scab.

Choosing Garden Tools

Very few tools are necessary for a small garden. It is better to buy a few simple, high-grade tools that will serve well for many years than equipment that is poorly designed or made of cheap or low-grade materials that will not last. In most instances, the only tools needed are a spade or spading fork, a steel bow rake, a 7-inch common hoe, a strong cord for laying off rows, a wheelbarrow, and a garden hose long enough to water all parts of the garden. A trowel can be useful in transplanting, but it is not essential. If the soil is properly prepared, plants can be set more easily with the hands alone than with a trowel.

For gardens that are from 2,000 to 4,000 square feet, a wheel hoe is very useful because it can be used for most work usually done with a common hoe and with much less effort. The single-wheel type is probably the easiest to handle and best for use as an all-purpose wheel hoe. Other styles are available and may be used if preferred.

The cultivating tools, or attachments, for the wheel hoe should include one or more of the so-called hoe blades. They are best for weeding and are used more than the cultivator teeth or small plow usually supplied with a wheel hoe.

For gardens over 4,000 square feet, a rotary garden tiller is useful in preparing the soil for planting and controlling weeds.

Many gardeners who do little or no farming have the choice of hiring equipment for garden-land preparation or buying their own. Equipment for hire too often is unavailable when needed, so that a favorable season for planting may be missed. Country gardeners, in increasing numbers, are turning to small farm and garden tractors for land preparation, cultivation, lawn mowing, and hauling sprayers in gardens and orchards. Those who garden every year and who have large homesteads usually find this equipment a good investment. The size and type of equipment needed depend on the amount of work to be done, the contour of the land, and the character of the soil. For cultivating and other light work a 2- to 3-horsepower tractor is used. If plowing or other heavy work is involved, a larger tractor is desirable. Modern outfits of this size are well adapted to cultivating small areas. A medium-size tractor suitable for cultivating a large garden can also be used for plowing.

The rotary tiller, which is capable of preparing light to medium soils for planting in one operation, has been widely adopted by gardeners who have such soils. In the hands of a careful operator and on land that is not too hard and heavy and is reasonably free from stones, roots, and other obstructions, this machine has many desirable features. It can be adjusted to cultivate very shallowly or to plow the soil and fit it for planting. Tools such as sweeps may be attached, thereby adapting the machine to straddle-row cultivating.

Use of well-adapted implements in preparing garden land greatly lessens the work required in cultivating. Clean, sharp, high-grade tools greatly lessen garden labor. For larger gardens, a wheel-type hand fertilizer distributor, a sprayer or duster (preferably a wheelbarrow-type power sprayer), and a seed drill are generally profitable. Minor tools include two pointed iron stakes and weeders.

If sufficient water is available, irrigation

equipment is necessary in many areas and highly desirable in nearly all gardens. Furrow application requires careful planning and laying out of the garden area and precise handling of the soil to insure even distribution of water. Overhead pipes with nozzles at short intervals, temporary lines of lightweight pipe with rotating sprinklers, and porous hose laid along the rows are extensively used. The most common practice is to use a length or two of garden hose, with or without sprinklers, fed by faucets on temporary or permanent lines of pipe through the garden.

In winter, when there is little heat from the sun, little water is used by plants so irrigation is not needed in most areas. However, in summer, rainfall is usually inadequate and irrigation is essential for maximum production.

Arranging the Garden

No one plan or arrangement for a garden can suit all conditions. Each gardener must plan to meet his own problem. Careful planning will lessen the work of gardening and increase the returns from the labor. Planting seeds and plants at random always results in waste and disappointment. Suggestions for planning a garden are here presented with the idea that they can be changed to suit the individual gardener.

The first consideration is whether the garden is to be in one unit or in two. With two plots, lettuce, radishes, beets, spinach, and other vegetables requiring little space are grown in a small kitchen garden, and potatoes, sweet corn, pumpkins, melons, and other vegetables requiring more room are planted in a separate patch, as between young-orchard-tree rows or in other areas where conditions are especially suitable for their culture.

The cultivation methods to be employed are important in planning the garden. When the work is to be done mainly with a garden tractor, the site and the arrangement should be such as to give the longest practicable rows. On slopes of more than 1½ percent, especially on light-textured soil, the rows should extend across the slope at right angles, or on the contours where the land is uneven. The garden should be free from paths across the rows, and turning spaces of 10 to 12 feet should be provided at the ends. The rows for small-growing crops may be closer together for hand cultivation than for cultivation with power equipment.

Any great variation in the composition of the soil within the garden should be taken into consideration when deciding on where to plant various crops. If part of the land is low and moist, such crops as celery, onions, and late cucumbers should be placed there. If part is high, warm, and dry, that is the proper spot for early crops, especially those needing a soil that warms up quickly.

Permanent crops, such as asparagus and rhubarb, should be planted where they will not interfere with the annual plowing of the garden and the cultivation of the annual crops. If a hotbed, a coldframe, or a special seedbed is provided, it should be either in one corner of, or outside, the garden.

Tall-growing crops should be planted where they will not shade or interfere with the growth of smaller crops. There seems to be little choice as to whether the rows do or do not run in a general east-and-west or in a general north-and-south direction, but they should conform to the contours of the land.

Succession of Crops

Except in dry-land areas, all garden space should be kept fully occupied throughout the growing season. In the South, this means the greater part of the year. In fact, throughout the South Atlantic and Gulf coast regions it is possible to have vegetables growing in the garden every month of the year.

In arranging the garden, all early-maturing crops may be grouped so that as soon as one crop is removed another takes its place. It is desirable, however, to follow a crop not with another of its kind, but with an unrelated crop. For example, early peas or beans can very properly be followed by late cabbage, celery, carrots, or beets; early corn or potatoes can be followed by fall turnips or spinach. It is not always necessary to wait until the early crop is entirely removed; a later one may be planted between the rows of the early crop—for example, sweet corn between potato rows. Crops subject to attack by the same diseases and insects should not follow each other.

In the extreme North, where the season is relatively short, there is very little opportunity for succession cropping. In dry-land areas, inter-cropping generally is not feasible, because of limited moisture supply. Therefore, plenty of land should be provided to accommodate the desired range and volume of garden crops.

Late Summer and Fall Garden

Although gardening is commonly considered mainly as a spring and early-summer enterprise, the late-summer and fall garden deserves attention too. Second and third plantings of crops adapted to growing late in the season not only provide a supply of fresh vegetables for the latter part of the season but often give better products for canning, freezing, and storing. Late-grown snap and lima beans and spinach, for example, are well adapted to freezing and canning; beets, carrots, celery, and turnips, to storage. In the South, the late-autumn garden is as important as the early-autumn one.

Selecting Seed

Except in special cases, it pays the gardener to buy seed from reputable seedsmen and not to depend on home-grown supplies. Very fine varieties that do extremely well in certain areas have been grown for long periods from locally produced seed, and such practices are to be commended, provided adequate measures are taken to keep the strains pure.

Vegetables that are entirely, or readily, cross-pollinated *among plants of their kind* include corn, cucumbers, melons, squash, pumpkins, cress, mustard, brussels sprouts, cabbage, cauliflower, collards, kale, kohlrabi, spinach, onion, radish, beet, and turnip. Those less readily cross-pollinated are eggplant, pepper, tomato, carrot, and celery. Beans, peas, okra, and lettuce are generally self-pollinated, but occasionally cross-pollinated, lima beans sometimes rather extensively. Because sweet corn will cross with field corn, it is unwise to save sweet corn seed if field corn is growing in the same neighborhood. Hybrid sweet corn should not be saved for seed. The custom of saving seed from a choice watermelon is safe, provided no citrons or other varieties of watermelons are growing nearby. Likewise, seed from a muskmelon is safe, even though it was grown side by side with cucumbers. Beans do not readily cross and their seed also may be saved. Cabbage, kohlrabi, kale, collards, broccoli, and cauliflower all intercross freely, so each must be well isolated from the others if seed is to be saved.

Seeds should be ordered well in advance of planting time, but only after the preparation of a garden plan that shows the size of the plantings and the quantity of seed required. Table 2 shows the quantity of seed required for a given space, but allowance should be made for the possible need of replanting. Crops and varieties that are known to be adapted to the locality should be selected. The agricultural experiment station of each State, county agricultural agents, and experienced gardeners are usually able to give advice about varieties of vegetables that are adapted to the area. Standard sorts of known quality and performance are usually the best choice.

Disease-resistant strains and varieties of many important vegetables are now so generally available that there is little reason for risking the loss of a crop through planting susceptible sorts. This phase of the subject is treated in detail under the individual crops.

Some seeds retain their vitality longer than others. Seeds may be divided into three groups as follows: (1) Comparatively short-lived, usually not good after 1 to 2 years—corn, leek, onion, parsley, parsnip, rhubarb and salsify; (2) moderately long-lived, often good for 3 to 5 years—asparagus, beans, brussels sprouts, cabbage, carrot, cauliflower, celery, kale, lettuce, okra, peas, pepper, radish, spinach, turnip and watermelon; and (3) long-lived, may be good for more than 5 years—beet, cucumber, eggplant, muskmelon, and tomato.

TABLE 2.—*Quantity of seed and number of plants required for 100 feet of row, depths of planting, and distances apart for rows and plants*

Crop	Requirement for 100 feet of row — Seed	Plants	Depth for planting seed	Rows — Horse- or tractor-cultivated	Hand-cultivated	Plants in the row
			Inches	*Feet*		
Asparagus	1 ounce	75	1 –1½	4 –5	1½ to 2 feet	18 inches.
Beans:						
Lima, bush	½ pound		1 –1½	2½–3	2 feet	3 to 4 inches.
Lima, pole	½ pound		1 –1½	3 –4	3 feet	3 to 4 inches.
Snap, bush	½ pound		1 –1½	2½–3	2 feet	3 to 4 inches.
Snap, pole	4 ounces		1 –1½	3 –4	2 feet	3 feet.
Beet	2 ounces		1	2 –2½	14 to 16 inches	2 to 3 inches.
Broccoli:						
Heading	1 packet	50– 75	½	2½–3	2 to 2½ feet	14 to 24 inches.
Sprouting	1 packet	50– 75	½	2½–3	2 to 2½ feet	14 to 24 inches.
Brussels sprouts	1 packet	50– 75	½	2½–3	2 to 2½ feet	14 to 24 inches.
Cabbage	1 packet	50– 75	½	2½–3	2 to 2½ feet	14 to 24 inches.
Cabbage, Chinese	1 packet		½	2 –2½	18 to 24 inches	8 to 12 inches.
Carrot	1 packet		½	2 –2½	14 to 16 inches	2 to 3 inches.
Cauliflower	1 packet	50– 75	½	2½–3	2 to 2½ feet	14 to 24 inches.
Celeriac	1 packet	200–250	⅛	2½–3	18 to 24 inches	4 to 6 inches.
Celery	1 packet	200–250	⅛	2½–3	18 to 24 inches	4 to 6 inches.
Chard	2 ounces		1	2 –2½	18 to 24 inches	6 inches.
Chervil	1 packet		½	2 –2½	14 to 16 inches	2 to 3 inches.
Chicory, witloof	1 packet		½	2 –2½	18 to 24 inches	6 to 8 inches.
Chives	1 packet		½	2½–3	14 to 16 inches	In clusters.
Collards	1 packet		½	3 –3½	18 to 24 inches	18 to 24 inches.
Cornsalad	1 packet		½	2½–3	14 to 16 inches	1 foot.
Corn, sweet	2 ounces		2	3 –3½	2 to 3 feet	Drills, 14 to 16 inches; hills, 2½ to 3 feet.
Cress Upland	1 packet		⅛– ¼	2 –2½	14 to 16 inches	2 to 3 inches.
Cucumber	1 packet		½	6 –7	6 to 7 feet	Drills, 3 feet; hills, 6 feet.
Dasheen	5 to 6 pounds	50	2 –3	3½–4	3½ to 4 feet	2 feet.
Eggplant	1 packet	50	½	3	2 to 2½ feet	3 feet.
Endive	1 packet		½	2½–3	18 to 24 inches	12 inches.
Fennel, Florence	1 packet		½	2½–3	18 to 24 inches	4 to 6 inches.
Garlic	1 pound		1 –2	2½–3	14 to 16 inches	2 to 3 inches.
Horseradish	Cuttings	50–75	2	3 –4	2 to 2½ feet	18 to 24 inches.
Kale	1 packet		½	2½–3	18 to 24 inches	12 to 15 inches.
Kohlrabi	1 packet		½	2½–3	14 to 16 inches	5 to 6 inches.
Leek	1 packet		½–1	2½–3	14 to 16 inches	2 to 3 inches.
Lettuce, head	1 packet	100	½	2½–3	14 to 16 inches	12 to 15 inches.
Lettuce, leaf	1 packet		½	2½–3	14 to 16 inches	6 inches.
Muskmelon	1 packet		1	6 –7	6 to 7 feet	Hills, 6 feet.
Mustard	1 packet		½	2½–3	14 to 16 inches	12 inches.
Okra	2 ounces		1 –1½	3 –3½	3 to 3½ feet	2 feet.
Onion:						
Plants		400	1 –2	2 –2½	14 to 16 inches	2 to 3 inches.
Seed	1 packet		½–1	2 –2½	14 to 16 inches	2 to 3 inches.
Sets	1 pound		1 –2	2 –2½	14 to 16 inches	2 to 3 inches.
Parsley	1 packet		⅛	2 –2½	14 to 16 inches	4 to 6 inches.
Parsley, turnip-rooted	1 packet		⅛– ¼	2 –2½	14 to 16 inches	2 to 3 inches.
Parsnip	1 packet		½	2 –2½	18 to 24 inches	2 to 3 inches.
Peas	½ pound		2 –3	2 –4	1½ to 3 feet	1 inch.
Pepper	1 packet	50–70	½	3 –4	2 to 3 feet	18 to 24 inches.
Physalis	1 packet		½	2 –2½	1½ to 2 feet	12 to 18 inches.
Potato	5 to 6 pounds, tubers		4	2½–3	2 to 2½ feet	10 to 18 inches.
Pumpkin	1 ounce		1 –2	5 –8	5 to 8 feet	3 to 4 feet.
Radish	1 ounce		½	2 –2½	14 to 16 inches	1 inch.
Rhubarb		25–35		3 –4	3 to 4 feet	3 to 4 feet.
Salsify	1 ounce		½	2 –2½	18 to 26 inches	2 to 3 inches.
Shallots	1 pound (cloves)		1 –2	2 –2½	12 to 18 inches	2 to 3 inches.
Sorrel	1 packet		½	2 –2½	18 to 24 inches	5 to 8 inches.
Soybean	½ to 1 pound		1 –1½	2½–3	24 to 30 inches	3 inches.
Spinach	1 ounce		½	2 –2½	14 to 16 inches	3 to 4 inches.
Spinach, New Zealand	1 ounce		1 –1½	3 –3½	3 feet	18 inches.

9

Crop	Requirement for 100 feet of row		Depth for planting seed	Distance apart		
	Seed	Plants		Rows		Plants in the row
				Horse- or tractor-cultivated	Hand-cultivated	
Squash:						
Bush ----------	½ ounce ----------	----------	1 –2	4 –5	4 to 5 feet ----------	Drills, 15 to 18 inches; hills, 4 feet.
Vine ----------	1 ounce ----------	----------	1 –2	8 –12	8 to 12 feet ----------	Drills, 2 to 3 feet; hills, 4 feet.
Sweetpotato ----------	5 pounds, bedroots --	75	2 –3	3 –3½	3 to 3½ feet -------	12 to 14 inches.
Tomato ----------	1 packet ----------	35–50	½	3 –4	2 to 3 feet ----------	1½ to 3 feet.
Turnip greens ----------	1 packet ----------	----------	¼– ½	2 –2½	14 to 16 inches -----	2 to 3 inches.
Turnips and rutabagas -------	½ ounce ----------	----------	¼– ½	2 –2½	14 to 16 inches -----	2 to 3 inches.
Watermelon ----------	1 ounce ----------	----------	1 –2	8 –10	8 to 10 feet ----------	Drills, 2 to 3 feet; hills, 8 feet.

Starting the Plants

Table 2 gives in general the proper depth of planting for seed of the various vegetables, the quantity of seed or number of plants required for 100 feet of row, and the correct spacing of rows and of plants within the row. Special planting suggestions are given in the cultural hints for the various garden crops.

Earliness, economy of garden space, and lengthening of the growing season may be obtained by setting the plants of many vegetables instead of sowing the seed directly in the garden. Moreover, it is almost impossible to establish good stands from seed sown directly in place in the garden with delicate plants, such as celery, under average conditions.

In the warmer parts of the United States, practically all vegetable plants may be started in specially prepared beds in the open with little or no covering. In the temperate and colder regions, if an early garden is desired, it is essential that certain crops, such as tomatoes, peppers, eggplant, early cabbage, cauliflower, and early head lettuce, be started indoors, in hotbeds, or in coldframes. Occasionally onion, beet, cucumber, squash, and melons are started under cover and transplanted.

Starting Plants in the House

Seeds can be germinated and seedlings started in a box, pan, or flowerpot of soil in a window. In addition to having at least 6 hours of direct sunlight each day, the room must be kept reasonably warm at all times.

Washed fine sand and shredded sphagnum moss are excellent media in which to start seeds. Place a layer of easily drained soil in the bottom of a flat and cover this soil with a layer —about three-fourths inch thick—of either fine sand or sphagnum moss. Press the sand or moss to form a smooth, firm seedbed.

Then, using a jig (fig. 4), make furrows in the seedbed one-half inch deep. Water the sand or moss thoroughly and allow it to drain.

Sow seeds thinly in the rows and cover the seeds lightly with a second layer of sand or moss. Sprinkle the flat, preferably with a fine mist, and cover the flat with a sheet of clear plastic film (fig. 5). The plastic film diffuses and subdues the light and holds moisture in the soil and air surrounding the seeds. Plastic films offer advantages over glass coverings in that they are light in weight and are nonshattering.

Place the seeded and covered flat in a location that is reasonably warm at all times and has 6 hours of direct sunlight each day. The flat will require no further attention until after the seedlings have developed their first true leaves (fig. 6). They are then ready to transplant to other containers.

It is seldom possible to keep the transplanted plants in house windows without their becoming spindling and weak. For healthy growth,

Figure 4.—One-half-inch furrows made with a jig.

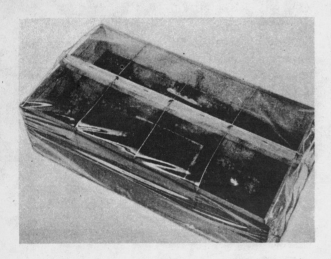

Figure 5.—Clear plastic film gives a flat, even, subdued light and holds the moisture.

place them in a hotbed, coldframe, or other place where they will receive an abundance of sunshine, ample ventilation, and a suitable temperature.

Strong, vigorous seedlings can be started under 40-watt fluorescent tubes (fig. 7). These tubes should be 6 to 8 inches above the seedlings. Temperatures should be about 60° F. at night and 70° during the day. Best results are obtained if the fluorescent fixture is next to a window to increase the amount of light reaching the young plants.

Soil pellets are the simplest and easiest method for starting plants and are readily available from garden supply stores and other sources. Soil pellets are a well-balanced synthetic soil mixture and are free of soilborne diseases and weeds (fig. 8).

Special Devices for Starting Plants

In determining the type of equipment for starting early plants, the gardener must consider the temperature and other climatic conditions in his locality, as well as the nature of the plants to be started. Hardy plants, such as cabbage, need only simple inexpensive facilities, but such heat-loving, tender seedlings as peppers and eggplant must have more elaborate facilities for successful production. In the warmer parts of the United States, and in the well-protected locations elsewhere, a coldframe or a sash-covered pit on the sunny side of a building usually suffices (fig. 9). In colder sections, or in exposed areas elsewhere, some form of artificial heat is essential. Where only a little protection against cold damage, at infrequent intervals, is needed, a coldframe in which a temporary bank of lamps can be placed may be sufficient. The hotbed, lean-to, or sash greenhouse heated by manure, pipes, flues, or electricity are all widely used, the choice depending on conditions. A comparatively small plant-growing structure will provide enough plants for several gardens, and joint efforts by a number of gardeners will usually reduce the labor of producing plants.

Figure 6.—Seedlings with first true leaves ready for transplanting.

11

Figure 7.—Starting plants under fluorescent light opposite a window.

Figure 8.—Soil pellets, left to right, unmoistened, moistened with emerging seedling, and lettuce plant ready to plant in the garden.

The plant-growing structure should always be on well-drained land free from danger of flooding. A sunny, southern exposure on a moderate slope, with trees, a hedge, a board fence, or other form of windbreak on the north and west, makes a desirable site. Plenty of sunshine is necessary.

Hotbeds and other plant-growing devices require close attention. They must be ventilated at frequent intervals, and the plants may require watering more than once daily. Convenience in handling the work is important. Sudden storms may necessitate closing the structure within a matter of minutes. Plant growing at home should not be undertaken by persons obliged to be away for extended periods, leaving the plant structure unattended.

A tight well-glazed structure is necessary where the climate is severe; less expensive facilities are satisfactory elsewhere.

Covers for hotbeds and coldframes may be glass sash, fiber glass, plastic film, muslin, or light canvas.

In the moderate and cooler sections of the country, standard 3- by 6-foot hotbed sash is most satisfactory. Even this requires supplementary covering with canvas, blankets, mats, or similar material during freezing weather. The amount of covering is determined by the degree of heat supplied the structure, the severity of the weather, and the kind of plants and their stage of development. Farther South, where less protection is necessary, a muslin cover may be all that is needed and for only a part of the time.

Many substitutes for glass as coverings for hotbeds and coldframes are on the market. The most widely used substitutes are various kinds of clear plastic film. Some of these have a lifespan of only one season, and others a lifespan of 3 to 5 years.

Clear plastic film transmits as much light as glass in the visible range, and more than glass in the ultraviolet and infrared ranges.

The film comes as flat sheets (on rolls) and in tubular form. Flat-sheet film is used for tack-

Figure 9.—Growing early plants in a glass coldframe located on the south side of the house. Some heat is applied from the basement window.

ing onto wooden frames; the tubular form is used for enclosing metal tubular frames with a tight double layer of film.

Large plant hoods made from semicircular aluminum or galvanized steel pipe and fitted with a sleeve of tubular plastic film (fig. 10) make excellent coldframes or seasonal row covers. When used in this way, a double layer of plastic film provides an air space that insulates against 4° to 7° of frost temperature change.

Electrically heated plant beds are ideal for the home gardener, provided electric rates are not too high. The beds may be built any size. Because they are equipped with thermostatic control, they require a minimum of attention. It is now possible to buy frames—completely equipped with heating cables, switches, and thermostats—ready to assemble and set in position. Fill the frames with soil or plant boxes and connect to a source of current (fig. 11).

Small frames may be removed at the end of the season and stored; larger frames are usually treated as a permanent installation.

Hardening Plants

Plants should be gradually hardened, or toughened, for 2 weeks before planting in the open garden. This is done by slowing down their rate of growth to prepare them to withstand such conditions as chilling, drying winds, shortage of water, or high temperatures. Cabbage, lettuce, onion, and many other plants can be hardened to withstand frost; others, such as tomatoes and peppers cannot. Withholding water and lowering the temperature are the best ways to harden a plant. This may be done in a glass or plastic coldframe.

About 10 days before being planted in the open ground, the young plants in beds or flats

Figure 10. A double layer of plastic film supported by semicircular galvanized pipe makes a highly satisfactory portable coldframe.

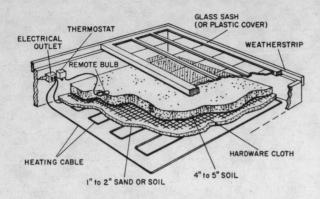

ELECTRICAL OUTLET — THERMOSTAT — GLASS SASH (OR PLASTIC COVER) — WEATHERSTRIP — REMOTE BULB — HEATING CABLE — 1" to 2" SAND OR SOIL — 4" to 5" SOIL — HARDWARE CLOTH

Figure 11.—An electrically heated glass hotbed with thermostatic control is ideal for the home gardener.

are blocked out with a large knife. Blocking, or cutting the roots, causes new roots to form quickly near the plants, making recovery from transplanting in the open easier. Blocking also makes it easier to remove the plants from the bed or flat with minimum injury.

Southern-Grown Plants

Vegetable plants grown outdoors in the South are shipped to all parts of the country. They are grown cheaply and usually withstand shipment and resetting very well. They may not always be as good as home-grown plants, but they save the trouble of starting them in the house or in a hot-bed. Plants of beets, brussels sprouts, cabbage, cauliflower, lettuce, onions, peppers, and tomatoes are extensively grown and shipped; tomato, cabbage, and onion plants make up the bulk of the shipments. The plants are usually wrapped in bundles of 50 each and shipped by either mail or express. Tomato and pepper plants are packed with a little damp moss around the roots, but onion and cabbage plants are usually packed with bare roots. Shipments involving large numbers of bundles are packed in ventilated hampers or slatted crates and usually are sent by motor-truck or rail express. Shipments by air mail and air express are increasing.

The disadvantages of using southern-grown plants are the occasional delays in obtaining them and the possibility of transmitting such diseases as the wilt disease of the tomato, black rot of cabbage, and disorders caused by nematodes. State-certified plants that have been care-fully inspected and found as free of these troubles as can be reasonably determined are available. Southern-grown plants are now offered for sale by most northern seedsmen, by mail-order houses, and often by local hardware and supply houses.

Transplanting

The term "transplanting" means shifting of a plant from one soil or culture medium to another. It may refer to the shifting of small seedlings from the seedbed to other containers where the plants will have more space for growth, or it may mean the setting of plants in the garden row where they are to develop for the crop period. Contrary to general belief, transplanting does not in itself stimulate the plant or make it grow better; actually growth is temporarily checked, but the plant is usually given more space in which to grow. Every effort should be made during transplanting to interrupt the growth of the plant as little as possible.

Plants started in seed flats, flowerpots, and other containers in the house, the hotbed, the greenhouse, or elsewhere should be shifted as soon as they can be handled to boxes, flowerpots, plant bands, or other containers where they will have more room to develop. If shifted to flats or similar containers, the plants should be spaced 2 or more inches apart. This provides room for growth until the plants can be moved to their permanent place in the garden. Most gardeners prefer to place seedlings singly in flowerpots, paper cups with the bottoms pierced for drainage, plant bands, berry boxes, or other containers. When the plants are set in the garden, the containers are carefully removed.

Soil for transplanting should be fertile, usually a mixture of rich topsoil and garden compost, with a very light addition of a commercial garden fertilizer.

Moistening the seedbed before removing the seedlings and care in lifting and separating the delicate plants make it possible to shift them with little damage to the root system and with only minor checks to their growth. Plants grown singly in separate containers can be moved to the garden with almost no disturbance to the root system, especially those that are hardened for a week or two before being set outdoors. Plants being hardened should be watered sparingly, but just before they are set out, they should be given a thorough soaking.

Plants grown in the hotbed or greenhouse without being shifted from the seedbed to provide more room and those shipped from the South usually have very little soil adhering to the roots when they are set in the garden. Such plants may require special care if transplanting conditions are not ideal; otherwise, they will die or at least suffer a severe shock that will greatly retard their development. The roots of these plants should be kept covered and not allowed to dry out. Dipping the roots in a mixture of clay and water helps greatly in bridging the critical transplanting period. Planting when the soil is moist also helps. Pouring a half pint to a pint of water, or less for small plants, into the hole around the plant before it is completely filled is usually necessary. A starter solution made by mixing ½ pound of a 4–12–4 or 5–10–5 commercial fertilizer in 4 gallons of water may be used instead of plain water. It is usually beneficial. Finally, the freshly set plants should be shaded for a day or two with newspapers.

Plants differ greatly in the way they recover from the loss of roots and from exposure to new conditions. Small plants of tomatoes, lettuce, beets, cabbage, and related vegetables are easy to transplant. They withstand the treatment better than peppers, eggplant, and the vine crops. When started indoors and moved to the field, the vine crops should be seeded directly in berry baskets or containers of the same size that can be transferred to the garden and removed without disturbing the root systems. Beans and sweet corn can be handled in the same manner, thereby often gaining a week or two in earliness.

Planting the Garden

One of the most important elements of success in growing vegetables is planting, or transplanting, each crop at the time or times that are best for the operation in each locality. Temperatures often differ so much between localities not many miles apart that the best planting dates for some one vegetable may differ by several days or even 2 weeks.

Vegetable crops may be roughly grouped and sown according to their hardiness and their temperature requirements. A rough timetable for planting some of the commoner crops is shown in table 3, based on the frost-free dates in spring and fall. The frost-free date in spring is usually 2 to 3 weeks later than the average date of the last freeze in a locality and is approximately the date that oak trees leaf out.

The gardener naturally wants to make the first planting of each vegetable as early as he can without too much danger of its being damaged by cold. Many vegetables are so hardy to cold that they can be planted a month or more before the average date of the last freeze, or about 6 weeks before the frost-free date. Furthermore, most, if not all, cold-tolerant crops actually thrive better in cool weather than in hot weather and should not be planted late in the spring in the southern two-thirds of the country where summers are hot. Thus, the gardener must time his planting not only to escape cold but with certain crops also to escape heat. Some vegetables that will not thrive when planted in late spring in areas having rather hot summers may be sown in late summer, however, so that they will make most of their growth in cooler weather.

TABLE 3.—*Some common vegetables grouped according to the approximate times they can be planted and their relative requirements for cool and warm weather*

Cold-hardy plants for early-spring planting		Cold-tender or heat-hardy plants for later-spring or early-summer planting			Hardy plants for late-summer or fall planting except in the North (plant 6 to 8 weeks before first fall freeze)
Very hardy (plant 4 to 6 weeks before frost-free date)	Hardy (plant 2 to 4 weeks before frost-free date)	Not cold-hardy (plant on frost-free date)	Requiring hot weather (plant 1 week or more after frost-free date)	Medium heat-tolerant (good for summer planting)	
Broccoli	Beets	Beans, snap	Beans, lima	Beans, all	Beets
Cabbage	Carrot	Okra	Eggplant	Chard	Collard
Lettuce	Chard	New Zealand spinach	Peppers	Soybean	Kale
Onions	Mustard	Soybean	Sweetpotato	New Zealand spinach	Lettuce
Peas	Parsnip	Squash	Cucumber	Squash	Mustard
Potato	Radish	Sweet corn	Melons	Sweet corn	Spinach
Spinach		Tomato			Turnip
Turnip					

A gardener anywhere in the United States can determine his own safe planting dates for different crops by using the maps (figs. 12 and 13), together with tables 4 and 5.

The maps show the average dates of the last killing frosts in spring and the average dates of the first killing frosts in fall. They are the dates from which planting times can be determined, and such determinations have been so worked out in tables 4 and 5 that any gardener can use them, with only a little trouble, to find out the planting dates for his locality.

Table 4, for use with the map in figure 12, shows planting dates between January 1 and June 30, covering chiefly spring and early-summer crops. It shows *how early it is safe to plant;* it also shows the spring and early-summer dates *beyond which planting usually gives poor results.*

Opposite each vegetable in table 4, the first date in any column is the *earliest generally safe* date that the crop can be sown or transplanted by the gardener using that column. (No gardener needs to use more than one of the columns.) The second date is the latest date that is likely to prove satisfactory for the planting. All times in between these two dates may not, however, give equally good results. Most of the crops listed do better when planted not too far from the earlier date shown.

To determine the best time to plant any vegetable in the spring in your locality:

1. Find your location on the map in figure 12 and then, the solid line on the map that comes nearest to it.

2. Find the date shown on the solid line. This is the average date of the last killing frost. The first number represents the month; the second number, the day. Thus, 3–10 is March 10. Once you know the date you are through with the map.

3. Turn to table 4; find the column that has your date over it; and draw a heavy line around this entire column. It is the only date column in the table that you will need.

4. Find the dates in the column that are on a line with the name of the crop you want to plant. These dates show the period during which the crop can safely be planted. The best time is on, or soon after, the first of the two dates. A time halfway between them is very good; the second date is not so good.

For areas in the Plains region that warm up quickly in the spring and are subject to dry weather, very early planting is essential to escape heat and drought. In fact, most of the cool-season crops do not thrive when spring-planted in the southern part of the Great Plains and southern Texas.

Table 5 is used with the map in figure 13 in the same way to find the dates for late plantings. The recommendations for late plantings and for those in the South for overwintered crops are less exact and less dependable than those for early planting. Factors other than direct temperature effects—summer rainfall, for example, and the severity of diseases and insects—often make success difficult, especially in the Southeast, although some other areas having the same frost dates are more favorable. A date about halfway between the two shown in table 5 will generally be best, although in most areas fair success can be expected within the entire range of dates shown.

Along the northern half of the Pacific coast, warm-weather crops should not be planted quite so late as the frost date and table would indicate. Although frost comes late, very cool weather prevails for some time before frost, retarding late growth of crops like sweet corn, lima beans, and tomatoes.

Caring for the Garden

Watering

In most areas the garden requires a moisture supply equivalent to about an inch of rain a week during the growing season for best plant growth. It requires roughly that amount of watering a week to maintain good production if the moisture stored in the soil becomes depleted and no rain falls over periods of weeks. An inch of rain is equivalent to about 28,000 gallons on an acre, or 900 gallons on a 30- by 50-foot garden.

MEAN DATE OF LAST 32° (F.) TEMPERATURE IN SPRING

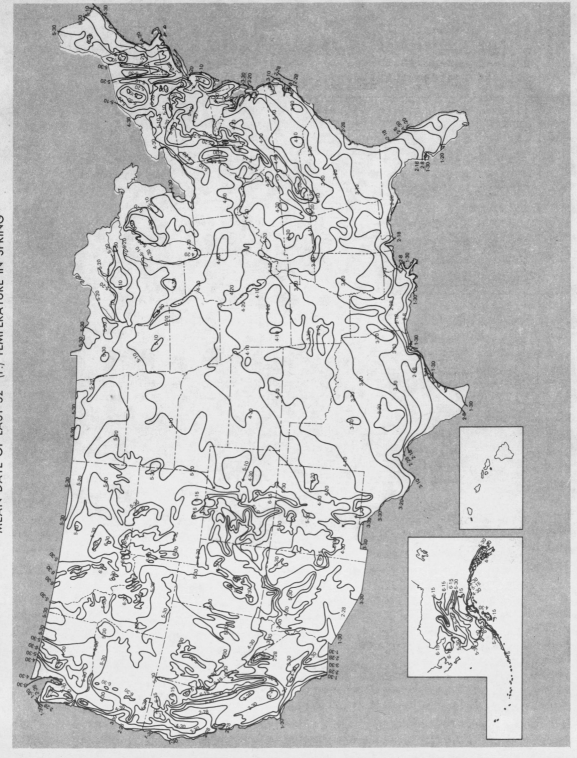

Figure 12.—Average dates of the last killing frost in spring.

TABLE 4.—*Earliest dates, and range of dates, for safe spring planting of vegetables in the open*

Crop	Planting dates for localities in which average date of last freeze is—						
	Jan. 30	Feb. 8	Feb. 18	Feb. 28	Mar. 10	Mar. 20	Mar. 30
Asparagus [1]	Feb. 1–Apr. 15	Feb. 10–May 1	Mar. 1–May 1	Mar. 15–June 15	Mar. 1	Feb. 1–Mar. 10	Feb. 15–Mar. 20.
Beans, lima	Feb. 1–Apr. 1	Feb. 1–May 1	Mar. 1–May 1	Mar. 15–June 15	Mar. 20–June 1	Apr. 1–June 15	Apr. 15–June 20.
Beans, snap	Jan. 1–Mar. 15	Jan. 1–Apr. 1	Jan. 1–Apr. 1	Feb. 1–Mar. 1	Mar. 15–May 15	Mar. 15–May 25	Apr. 1–June 1.
Beet	Jan. 1–30	Jan. 1–30	Jan. 1–Mar. 1	Jan. 1–Mar. 1	Feb. 15–Mar. 15	Feb. 15–Mar. 15	Mar. 1–June 1.
Broccoli, sprouting [1]	Jan. 1–30	Jan. 1–30	Jan. 1–Mar. 1	Jan. 1–Mar. 1	Feb. 15–Mar. 15	Feb. 15–Mar. 15	Mar. 1–20.
Brussels sprouts [1]	Jan. 1–15	Jan. 1–30	Jan. 1–30	Jan. 1–Mar. 1	Jan. 25–Mar. 1	Feb. 1–Mar. 1	Feb. 15–Mar. 10.
Cabbage [1]	(2)	Jan. 1–15	Jan. 1–Feb. 25	Jan. 15–Feb. 25	Jan. 25–Mar. 1	Feb. 1–Mar. 1	Feb. 15–Mar. 10.
Cabbage, Chinese	Jan. 1–Mar. 1	Jan. 1–Mar. 1	(2)	(2)	(2)	(2)	(2)
Carrot	Jan. 1–Feb. 1	Jan. 1–Mar. 1	Jan. 15–Feb. 15	Jan. 1–Mar. 1	Feb. 10–Mar. 15	Feb. 15–Mar. 20	Mar. 1–Apr. 10.
Cauliflower [1]	Jan. 1–Feb. 1	Jan. 1–Feb. 1	Jan. 10–Feb. 10	Jan. 20–Feb. 20	Feb. 1–Mar. 1	Feb. 10–Mar. 10	Feb. 20–Mar. 20.
Celery and celeriac	Jan. 1–Feb. 1	Jan. 1–Feb. 10	Jan. 20–Feb. 20	Feb. 20–Mar. 20	Feb. 20–May 20	Mar. 1–Apr. 1	Feb. 15–Apr. 15.
Chard	Jan. 1–Apr. 1	Jan. 1–Apr. 15	Jan. 20–Apr. 15	Feb. 1–May 1	Feb. 15–May 15	Feb. 20–May 20	Mar. 1–May 25.
Chervil and chives	(2)	(2)	(2)	Jan. 1–Feb. 1	Jan. 1–Apr. 1	Feb. 1–Apr. 1	Feb. 15–Mar. 15.
Chicory, witloof	—	—	—	—	June 1–July 1	June 1–July 1	June 1–July 1.
Collards [1]	Jan. 1–Feb. 15	Jan. 1–Feb. 15	Jan. 1–Mar. 15	Jan. 1–Mar. 15	Jan. 1–Mar. 15	Jan. 1–Mar. 15	Jan. 15–Mar. 15.
Cornsalad	Jan. 1–Feb. 15	Jan. 1–Feb. 15	Jan. 1–Mar. 1	Jan. 1–Mar. 1	Jan. 1–Mar. 15	Jan. 15–Mar. 15	Mar. 25–May 15.
Corn, sweet	Feb. 1–Mar. 15	Feb. 1–Apr. 15	Feb. 20–Apr. 15	Mar. 1–Apr. 15	Mar. 10–Apr. 15	Mar. 15–May 15	Mar. 1–Apr. 1.
Cress, upland	Jan. 1–Feb. 15	Jan. 1–Feb. 15	Jan. 15–Feb. 15	Jan. 15–Feb. 15	Feb. 1–Mar. 1	Feb. 20–Mar. 15	Apr. 10–May 15.
Cucumber	Feb. 15–Mar. 15	Feb. 15–Apr. 15	Feb. 15–Apr. 15	Mar. 1–Apr. 15	Mar. 15–Apr. 15	Apr. 1–May 1	Mar. 15–Apr. 15.
Eggplant [1]	Feb. 1–Mar. 1	Feb. 10–Apr. 15	Feb. 20–Apr. 15	Mar. 10–Apr. 15	Mar. 15–Apr. 15	Apr. 1–May 1	Apr. 10–May 15.
Endive	Jan. 1–Mar. 1	Jan. 1–Mar. 1	Jan. 1–Mar. 1	Jan. 1–Mar. 1	Feb. 15–Mar. 15	Feb. 20–Mar. 15	Mar. 15–Apr. 15.
Fennel, Florence	Jan. 1–Mar. 1	Jan. 1–Mar. 1	Jan. 15–Mar. 1	Feb. 1–Mar. 1	Feb. 15–Mar. 15	Apr. 1–May 1	Apr. 10–May 10.
Garlic	(2)	(2)	(2)	(2)	(2)	(2)	(2)
Horseradish [1]	—	Jan. 1–Feb. 1	Jan. 20–Feb. 20	Feb. 1–20	Feb. 10–Mar. 10	Feb. 20–Mar. 10	Mar. 10–Apr. 10.
Kale	Jan. 1–Feb. 1	Jan. 1–Feb. 1	Jan. 1–Feb. 1	Feb. 1–20	Feb. 10–Mar. 10	Feb. 20–Mar. 10	Feb. 10–Mar. 10.
Kohlrabi	Jan. 1–Feb. 1	Jan. 1–Feb. 1	Jan. 1–Feb. 15	Jan. 15–Feb. 15	Feb. 1–Mar. 1	Feb. 20–Mar. 10	Mar. 1–Apr. 1.
Leek	Jan. 1–Feb. 1	Jan. 1–Feb. 1	Jan. 1–Feb. 1	Jan. 1–Feb. 1	Jan. 25–Mar. 1	Feb. 1–Apr. 1	Mar. 1–20.
Lettuce, head [1]	Jan. 1–Feb. 1	Jan. 1–Feb. 1	Jan. 1–Feb. 15	Jan. 15–Feb. 15	Jan. 15–Mar. 10	Feb. 15–Mar. 15	Mar. 1–20.
Lettuce, leaf	Jan. 1–Feb. 1	Jan. 1–Mar. 1	Jan. 1–Mar. 1	Jan. 1–Mar. 1	Jan. 1–Mar. 1	Jan. 20–Mar. 1	Mar. 15–Apr. 15.
Muskmelon	Feb. 15–Mar. 15	Feb. 15–Apr. 1	Feb. 15–Apr. 15	Mar. 1–Apr. 1	Mar. 15–Apr. 15	Apr. 1–May 1	Apr. 15–May 15.
Mustard	Jan. 1–Mar. 1	Jan. 1–Mar. 1	Jan. 1–Mar. 1	Jan. 1–Mar. 1	Feb. 1–Mar. 1	Feb. 10–Mar. 20	Apr. 10–June 15.
Okra	Feb. 15–Apr. 1	Feb. 15–Apr. 15	Feb. 15–Apr. 15	Mar. 1–June 1	Mar. 20–June 1	Apr. 1–June 15	Apr. 10–June 15.
Onion [1]	Jan. 1–15	Jan. 1–15	Jan. 1–15	Jan. 1–Feb. 15	Feb. 1–Mar. 1	Feb. 15–Mar. 15	Feb. 15–Apr. 1.
Onion, seed	Jan. 1–15	Jan. 1–15	Jan. 1–15	Jan. 1–Feb. 15	Feb. 1–Mar. 1	Feb. 20–Mar. 15	Feb. 20–Mar. 15.
Onion, sets	Jan. 1–15	Jan. 1–15	Jan. 1–Mar. 1	Jan. 1–Mar. 15	Jan. 15–Mar. 10	Feb. 1–Mar. 20	Feb. 15–Mar. 20.
Parsley	Jan. 1–30	Jan. 1–30	Jan. 1–30	Jan. 15–Mar. 1	Feb. 1–Mar. 10	Feb. 15–Mar. 15	Mar. 1–Apr. 1.
Parsnip	—	—	Jan. 1–Mar. 1	Jan. 1–Mar. 1	Feb. 1–Mar. 10	Feb. 10–Mar. 15	Mar. 1–Apr. 1.
Peas, garden	Jan. 1–Feb. 15	Jan. 1–Feb. 15	Jan. 1–Mar. 1	Jan. 1–Mar. 1	Jan. 15–Mar. 15	Feb. 10–Mar. 15	Feb. 10–Mar. 15.
Peas, black-eye	Feb. 15–May 1	Feb. 15–May 15	Mar. 1–May 15	Mar. 10–June 15	Mar. 15–July 1	Apr. 1–June 1	Apr. 15–July 1.
Pepper [1]	Feb. 15–Apr. 1	Feb. 15–Apr. 15	Mar. 1–May 1	Mar. 15–May 1	Apr. 1–June 1	Apr. 10–June 1	Apr. 15–June 1.
Potato [1]	Jan. 1–Feb. 15	Jan. 1–Feb. 15	Jan. 1–Feb. 15	Jan. 15–Mar. 1	Feb. 1–Mar. 1	Feb. 10–Mar. 15	Feb. 20–Mar. 20.
Radish	Jan. 1–Apr. 1	Jan. 1–Apr. 1	Jan. 1–Apr. 1	Jan. 1–Apr. 1	Jan. 1–Apr. 1	Feb. 1–May 1	Feb. 15–May 1.
Rhubarb [1]	—	—	—	—	—	—	—
Rutabaga	—	Jan. 1–Feb. 1	Jan. 15–Feb. 15	Jan. 15–Mar. 1	Feb. 1–Mar. 1	Jan. 20–Mar. 1	Feb. 1–Mar. 1.
Salsify	Jan. 1–Feb. 15	Jan. 1–Feb. 15	Jan. 15–Feb. 20	Jan. 15–Mar. 1	Feb. 1–Mar. 1	Feb. 15–Mar. 1	Mar. 1–15.
Shallot	Jan. 1–Feb. 15	Jan. 1–Feb. 15	Jan. 15–Mar. 1	Jan. 15–Mar. 1	Feb. 10–Mar. 15	Feb. 15–Mar. 10	Feb. 15–Mar. 15.
Sorrel	Jan. 1–Mar. 1	Jan. 1–Mar. 1	Jan. 15–Mar. 1	Feb. 1–Mar. 10	Feb. 10–Mar. 15	Feb. 20–Mar. 20	Feb. 20–Apr. 15.
Soybean	Mar. 1–June 30	Mar. 1–June 30	Mar. 10–June 30	Mar. 20–June 30	Apr. 10–June 30	Apr. 10–June 20	Apr. 20–June 30.
Spinach	Jan. 1–Feb. 15	Jan. 1–Feb. 15	Jan. 1–Mar. 1	Jan. 1–Mar. 1	Jan. 15–Feb. 15	Jan. 15–Mar. 1	Feb. 1–Mar. 20.
Spinach, New Zealand	Feb. 1–Apr. 15	Feb. 15–Apr. 15	Mar. 1–Apr. 15	Mar. 15–May 15	Mar. 20–May 15	Apr. 1–June 15	Apr. 1–June 1.
Squash, summer	Feb. 15–Apr. 15	Feb. 15–Apr. 15	Mar. 1–Apr. 15	Mar. 15–May 15	Mar. 15–May 15	Apr. 1–May 15	Apr. 10–June 1.
Sweetpotato	Mar. 1–...	Mar. 1–...	Mar. 1–June 1	Mar. 20–June 1	Apr. 1–June 1	Apr. 10–June 1	Apr. 20–June 1.
Tomato	Feb. 15–Apr. 15	Feb. 20–Apr. 10	Mar. 1–Apr. 1	Mar. 10–May 1	Mar. 20–May 10	Apr. 1–May 20	Apr. 10–June 1.
Turnip	Jan. 1–Mar. 1	Jan. 1–Mar. 1	Jan. 10–Mar. 1	Jan. 20–Mar. 1	Feb. 1–Mar. 1	Feb. 10–Mar. 10	Feb. 20–Mar. 20.
Watermelon	Feb. 15–Apr. 15	Feb. 15–Apr. 1	Feb. 15–Apr. 15	Mar. 1–Apr. 15	Mar. 15–Apr. 15	Apr. 1–May 1	Apr. 10–May 15.

[1] Plants.
[2] Generally fall-planted (table 5).

TABLE 4.—Earliest dates, and range of dates, for safe spring planting of vegetables in the open—Continued

Crop	Planting dates for localities in which average date of last freeze is—						
	Apr. 10	Apr. 20	Apr. 30	May 10	May 20	May 30	June 10
Asparagus[1]	Mar. 10–Apr. 10	Mar. 15–Apr. 15	Mar. 20–Apr. 15	Mar. 10–Apr. 30	Apr. 20–May 15	May 1–June 1	May 15–June 1.
Beans, lima	Apr. 1–June 30	Apr. 1–June 20	May 15–June 15	May 25–June 15	May 15–June 15	May 25–June 15	May 15–June 15.
Beans, snap	Apr. 10–June 30	Apr. 25–June 30	May 10–June 30	May 10–June 30	May 10–June 15	May 1–June 15	May 20–June 10.
Beet	Mar. 10–June 1	Mar. 20–June 1	Apr. 1–June 15	Apr. 15–June 15	Apr. 25–June 15	May 1–June 15	May 20–June 10.
Broccoli, sprouting[1]	Mar. 15–Apr. 15	Mar. 25–Apr. 20	Apr. 1–June 15	Apr. 15–June 1	May 1–June 1	May 1–June 1	May 20–June 10.
Brussels sprouts[1]	Mar. 15–Apr. 15	Mar. 25–Apr. 20	Apr. 1–June 15	Apr. 15–June 1	May 1–June 1	May 1–June 1	May 20–June 10.
Cabbage[1]	Mar. 1–Apr. 1	Mar. 10–Apr. 1	Mar. 15–Apr. 10	Apr. 1–May 15	May 1–June 15	May 10–June 15	May 20–June 1.
Cabbage, Chinese	(²)	(²)	(²)	Apr. 1–May 15	May 1–June 15	May 10–June 15	May 20–June 1.
Carrot	Mar. 10–Apr. 20	Apr. 1–May 15	Apr. 10–June 1	Apr. 20–June 15	May 1–June 1	May 10–June 1	June 1–June 1.
Cauliflower[1]	Mar. 1–Mar. 20	Apr. 15–June 1	(²)	Apr. 20–June 15	Apr. 15–June 15	May 10–June 15	June 1–June 1.
Celery and celeriac	Apr. 1–Apr. 20	Apr. 10–May 1	Apr. 15–May 1	May 1–May 15	May 10–June 15	May 20–June 1	June 1–June 15.
Chard	Mar. 15–June 15	Apr. 1–June 15	Apr. 15–June 15	Apr. 20–June 15	May 10–June 15	May 20–June 1	June 1–June 15.
Chervil and chives	Mar. 1–Apr. 1	Mar. 10–Apr. 10	Mar. 15–Apr. 20	Apr. 1–May 1	Apr. 15–May 15	May 1–June 1	May 15–June 1.
Chicory, witloof	June 1–July 1	June 10–July 1	June 15–July 1	June 1–July 1	June 1–July 1	June 1–15	June 1–15.
Collards[1]	Mar. 1–June 1	Mar. 10–June 1	Apr. 1–June 1	Apr. 15–June 1	Apr. 1–June 1	May 1–June 1	May 15–June 1.
Cornsalad	Feb. 1–Apr. 1	Feb. 15–Apr. 15	Mar. 1–June 1	Apr. 15–June 1	Mar. 1–June 1	May 10–June 15	June 1–15.
Corn, sweet	Apr. 10–June 1	Apr. 25–June 15	May 10–June 15	May 10–June 15	May 15–June 15	May 1–June 15	May 15–June 15.
Cress, upland	Mar. 10–Apr. 15	Mar. 20–May 1	Apr. 10–May 10	Apr. 20–May 20	Apr. 10–May 10	Apr. 20–May 20	May 15–June 15.
Cucumber	Apr. 20–June 1	May 1–June 15	May 15–June 15	May 20–June 15	June 1–June 15	June 1–15	June 15.
Eggplant[1]	May 1–June 1	May 10–June 1	May 15–June 10	May 20–June 15	June 1–15	June 1–15	June 1–15.
Endive	Mar. 15–Apr. 15	Apr. 15–Apr. 15	Apr. 1–May 1	Apr. 15–May 15	May 1–30	May 1–30	May 15–June 1.
Fennel, Florence	Mar. 15–Apr. 15	Apr. 1–Apr. 15	Apr. 1–May 1	Apr. 15–May 15	May 1–30	May 1–30	May 15–June 1.
Garlic	Feb. 20–Mar. 20	Mar. 10–Apr. 1	Mar. 15–Apr. 15	Apr. 1–May 1	Apr. 15–May 15	May 1–30	May 15–June 1.
Horseradish[1]	Mar. 10–Apr. 10	Mar. 10–Apr. 10	Apr. 1–30	Apr. 1–30	Apr. 20–May 20	May 1–30	May 15–June 1.
Kale	Mar. 10–Apr. 1	Mar. 20–Apr. 10	Apr. 1–20	Apr. 10–May 10	Apr. 20–May 20	May 1–30	May 1–15.
Kohlrabi	Mar. 10–Apr. 10	Mar. 20–May 1	Apr. 1–May 1	Apr. 15–May 15	Apr. 20–May 20	May 1–30	May 1–15.
Leek	Mar. 1–Apr. 1	Mar. 15–Apr. 15	Apr. 1–May 1	Apr. 1–May 1	May 1–May 20	May 1–15	May 1–15.
Lettuce, head[1]	Mar. 10–Apr. 1	Mar. 20–Apr. 15	Apr. 1–May 1	Apr. 15–June 1	Apr. 15–June 1	May 1–30	May 20–June 30.
Lettuce, leaf	Mar. 15–May 15	Mar. 20–May 15	Apr. 1–June 1	Apr. 15–June 1	May 1–June 30	May 1–June 30	May 20–June 30.
Muskmelon	Apr. 20–June 1	May 1–June 15	May 15–June 15	May 15–June 15	June 1–June 15	May 1–15	—
Mustard	Mar. 10–Apr. 20	Mar. 20–May 1	Apr. 1–May 10	Apr. 15–June 1	May 1–June 30	May 10–June 30	May 20–June 30.
Okra	Apr. 20–June 15	May 1–June 1	May 1–June 10	May 20–June 10	June 1–20	June 1–20	June 1–20.
Onion[1]	Mar. 1–Apr. 1	Mar. 15–Apr. 10	Apr. 1–May 1	Apr. 1–May 1	Apr. 20–May 15	May 1–30	May 10–June 10.
Onion, seed	Mar. 1–Apr. 1	Mar. 15–Apr. 1	Apr. 1–15	Apr. 1–May 1	Apr. 20–May 15	May 1–30	May 10–June 10.
Onion, sets	Mar. 1–Apr. 1	Mar. 10–Apr. 1	Apr. 1–15	Apr. 1–May 1	Apr. 20–May 15	May 1–30	May 10–June 10.
Parsley	Mar. 10–Apr. 10	Mar. 20–Apr. 20	Apr. 1–May 1	Apr. 15–May 15	Apr. 20–May 20	May 1–30	May 10–June 10.
Parsnip	Mar. 10–Apr. 10	Mar. 20–May 1	Apr. 1–May 1	Apr. 15–June 1	May 1–June 1	May 10–June 1	May 20–June 15.
Peas, garden	Feb. 20–Mar. 20	Mar. 10–Apr. 1	Mar. 20–May 1	Apr. 1–May 15	Apr. 15–June 1	May 1–June 15	May 10–June 15.
Peas, black-eye	May 1–July 1	May 10–July 1	May 15–June 15	May 25–June 15	Apr. 15–June 15	—	—
Pepper[1]	May 1–June 1	May 10–June 1	May 15–June 10	May 20–June 15	May 25–June 15	Apr. 20–June 15	May 15–June 1.
Potato	Mar. 10–Apr. 1	Mar. 15–Apr. 10	Mar. 20–May 10	Apr. 1–June 1	Apr. 15–June 15	May 1–June 15	May 15–June 1.
Radish	Mar. 1–May 1	Mar. 10–May 10	Mar. 20–May 20	Apr. 1–June 1	Apr. 15–June 15	May 1–June 15	May 1–June 15.
Rhubarb[1]	Mar. 1–Apr. 1	Mar. 10–May 1	Mar. 20–May 10	Apr. 1–June 1	Apr. 15–May 10	May 1–20	May 1–June 1.
Rutabaga	—	—	May 1–June 1	May 1–June 1	May 1–20	May 10–20	May 20–June 10.
Salsify	Mar. 10–Apr. 15	Mar. 20–May 1	Apr. 1–June 1	Apr. 15–June 1	May 1–June 1	May 10–20	—
Shallot	Mar. 1–Apr. 1	Mar. 15–Apr. 15	Apr. 1–May 1	Apr. 1–June 1	Apr. 20–June 1	May 1–June 1	—
Sorrel	Mar. 1–Apr. 15	Mar. 15–May 1	Apr. 1–May 15	Apr. 15–June 1	May 1–June 1	May 10–June 1	May 1–June 1.
Soybean	May 15–June 15	May 25–June 10	May 10–June 10	May 15–June 10	May 1–June 10	May 10–June 15	—
Spinach	Feb. 15–Apr. 1	Mar. 1–Apr. 15	Mar. 15–Apr. 20	Apr. 1–June 15	Apr. 20–June 15	Apr. 20–June 15	May 1–June 15.
Spinach, New Zealand	Apr. 20–June 1	May 1–June 15	May 1–June 15	May 25–June 15	—	—	—
Squash, summer	May 1–May 15	May 1–30	May 1–30	May 10–June 10	May 20–June 15	June 1–20	June 10–20.
Sweetpotato	Apr. 20–June 1	May 10–June 10	May 20–June 10	May 20–June 10	Apr. 20–May 15	Apr. 20–June 15	—
Tomato	Mar. 1–Apr. 1	Mar. 10–May 1	Apr. 1–May 20	Apr. 20–June 1	May 1–June 1	May 5–20	June 15–30.
Turnip	Apr. 1–June 1	Apr. 10–May 1	Apr. 1–June 15	Apr. 15–June 1	Apr. 15–June 1	June 1–June 15	June 15–30.
Watermelon	Apr. 20–June 1	May 1–June 15	May 15–June 15	June 1–June 15	June 15–July 1	May 1–June 15	May 15–June 15.

[1] Plants.
[2] Generally fall-planted (table 5).

TABLE 5.—*Latest dates, and range of dates, for safe fall planting of vegetables in the open*

Crop	Planting dates for localities in which average dates of first freeze is—					
	Aug. 30	Sept. 10	Sept. 20	Sept. 30	Oct. 10	Oct. 20
Asparagus [1]				June 1–15	Oct. 20–Nov. 15	Nov. 1–Dec. 15.
Beans, lima				June 1–15	June 1–15	June 15–30.
Beans, snap		May 15–June 15	June 1–July 1	June 1–July 10	June 15–July 20	July 1–Aug. 1.
Beet	May 15–June 15	May 15–June 15	June 1–July 1	June 1–July 10	June 15–July 25	July 1–Aug. 5.
Broccoli, sprouting	May 1–June 1	May 1–June 1	May 1–June 15	June 1–30	June 15–July 15	July 1–Aug. 1.
Brussels sprouts	May 1–June 1	May 1–June 1	May 1–June 15	June 1–30	June 15–July 15	July 1–Aug. 1.
Cabbage [1]	May 1–June 1	May 1–June 1	May 1–June 15	June 1–July 10	June 1–July 15	July 1–20.
Cabbage, Chinese	May 15–June 15	May 15–June 15	June 1–July 1	June 1–July 15	June 15–Aug. 1	July 15–Aug. 15.
Carrot	May 15–June 15	May 15–June 15	June 1–July 1	June 1–July 10	June 1–July 20	June 15–Aug. 1.
Cauliflower [1]	May 1–June 1	May 1–July 1	May 1–July 1	May 10–July 15	June 1–July 25	July 1–Aug. 5.
Celery [1] and celeriac	May 1–June 1	May 15–June 15	May 15–July 1	June 1–July 5	June 1–July 15	June 1–Aug. 1.
Chard	May 15–June 15	May 15–July 1	June 1–July 1	June 1–July 5	June 1–July 20	June 1–Aug. 1.
Chervil and chives	May 10–June 10	May 1–June 15	May 15–June 15	(²)	(²)	(²)
Chicory, witloof	May 15–June 15	May 15–June 15	May 15–June 15	June 1–July 1	June 1–July 1	June 15–July 15.
Collards [1]	May 15–June 15	May 15–June 15	May 15–June 15	June 15–July 15	July 1–Aug. 1	July 15–Aug. 15.
Cornsalad	May 15–June 15	May 15–July 1	June 15–Aug. 1	July 15–Sept. 1	Aug. 15–Sept. 15	Sept. 1–Oct. 15.
Corn, sweet			June 1–July 1	June 1–July 1	June 1–July 10	June 1–July 20.
Cress, upland	May 15–June 15	May 15–July 1	June 15–Aug. 1	July 15–Sept. 1	Aug. 15–Sept. 15	Sept. 1–Oct. 15.
Cucumber			June 1–15	June 1–July 1	June 1–July 1	June 1–July 15.
Eggplant [1]				May 20–June 10	May 15–June 15	June 1–July 1.
Endive	June 1–July 1	June 1–July 1	June 15–July 15	June 15–Aug. 1	July 1–Aug. 15	July 15–Sept. 1.
Fennel, Florence	May 15–June 15	May 15–July 15	June 1–July 1	June 1–July 1	June 15–July 15	June 1–Aug. 1.
Garlic	(²)	(²)	(²)	(²)	(²)	(²)
Horseradish [1]	(²)	(²)	(²)	(²)	(²)	(²)
Kale	May 15–June 15	May 15–June 15	June 1–July 1	June 15–July 15	July 1–Aug. 1	July 15–Aug. 15.
Kohlrabi	May 15–June 15	June 1–July 1	June 1–July 15	June 15–July 15	July 1–Aug. 1	July 15–Aug. 15.
Leek	May 1–June 1	May 1–June 1	(²)	(²)	(²)	(²)
Lettuce, head [1]	May 15–July 1	May 15–July 1	June 1–July 15	June 15–Aug. 1	July 15–Aug. 15	Aug. 1–30.
Lettuce, leaf	May 15–July 15	May 15–July 15	June 1–Aug. 1	June 1–Aug. 1	July 15–Sept. 1	July 15–Sept. 1.
Muskmelon			May 1–June 15	May 15–June 1	June 1–June 15	June 15–July 20.
Mustard	May 15–July 15	May 15–July 15	June 1–Aug. 1	June 15–Aug. 1	July 15–Aug. 15	Aug. 1–Sept. 1.
Okra			June 1–20	June 1–July 1	June 1–July 15	June 1–Aug. 1.
Onion [1]	May 1–June 10	May 1–June 10	(²)	(²)	(²)	(²)
Onion, seed	May 1–June 1	May 1–June 10	(²)	(²)	(²)	(²)
Onion, sets	May 1–June 1	May 1–June 10	(²)	(²)	(²)	(²)
Parsley	May 15–June 15	May 1–June 15	June 1–July 1	June 1–July 15	June 15–Aug. 1	July 15–Aug. 15.
Parsnip	May 15–June 1	May 1–June 15	May 15–June 15	June 1–July 1	June 1–July 10	(²)
Peas, garden	May 10–June 15	May 1–July 1	June 1–July 15	June 1–Aug. 1	(²)	(²)
Peas, black-eye					June 1–July 1	June 1–July 1.
Pepper [1]			June 1–June 20	June 1–July 1	June 1–July 1	June 1–July 10.
Potato	May 15–June 1	May 1–June 15	May 1–June 15	May 1–June 15	May 15–June 15	June 15–July 15.
Radish	May 1–July 15	May 1–Aug. 1	June 1–Aug. 15	July 1–Sept. 1	July 15–Sept. 15	Aug. 1–Oct. 1.
Rhubarb [1]	Sept. 1–Oct. 1	Sept. 15–Oct. 15	Sept. 15–Nov. 1	Oct. 1–Nov. 1	Oct. 15–Nov. 15	Oct. 15–Dec. 1.
Rutabaga	May 15–June 15	May 1–June 15	June 1–July 1	June 1–July 1	June 15–July 15	July 10–20.
Salsify	May 15–June 1	May 10–June 10	May 20–June 20	June 1–20	June 1–July 1	June 1–July 1.
Shallot	(²)	(²)	(²)	(²)	(²)	(²)
Sorrel	May 15–June 15	May 15–June 15	June 1–July 1	June 1–July 15	July 1–Aug. 1	July 15–Aug. 15.
Soybean				May 25–June 10	June 1–25	June 1–July 5.
Spinach	May 15–July 1	June 1–July 15	June 1–Aug. 1	July 1–Aug. 15	Aug. 1–Sept. 1	Aug. 20–Sept. 10.
Spinach, New Zealand				May 15–July 1	June 1–July 15	June 1–Aug. 1.
Squash, summer	June 10–20	June 1–20	May 15–July 1	June 1–July 1	June 1–July 15	June 1–July 20.
Squash, winter			May 20–June 10	June 1–15	June 1–July 1	June 1–July 1.
Sweetpotato					May 20–June 10	June 1–15.
Tomato	June 20–30	June 10–20	June 1–20	June 1–20	June 1–20	June 1–July 1.
Turnip	May 15–June 15	June 1–July 1	June 1–July 15	June 1–Aug. 1	July 1–Aug. 1	July 15–Aug. 15.
Watermelon			May 1–June 15	May 15–June 1	June 1–June 15	June 15–July 20.

[1] Plants.
[2] Generally spring-planted (table 4).

Crop	Planting dates for localities in which average date of first freeze is—					
	Oct. 30	Nov. 10	Nov. 20	Nov. 30	Dec. 10	Dec. 20
Asparagus [1]	Nov. 15–Jan. 1	Dec. 1–Jan. 1				
Beans, lima	July 1–Aug. 1	July 1–Aug. 15	July 15–Sept. 1	Aug. 1–Sept. 15	Sept. 1–30	Sept. 1–Oct. 1.
Beans, snap	July 1–Aug. 15	July 1–Sept. 1	July 1–Sept. 10	Aug. 15–Sept. 20	Sept. 1–30	Sept. 1–Nov. 1.
Beet	Aug. 1–Sept. 1	Aug. 1–Oct. 1	Sept. 1–Dec. 1	Sept. 1–Dec. 15	Sept. 1–Dec. 31	Sept. 1–Dec. 31.
Broccoli, sprouting	July 1–Aug. 15	Aug. 1–Sept. 1	Aug. 1–Sept. 15	Aug. 1–Oct. 1	Aug. 1–Nov. 1	Sept. 1–Dec. 31.
Brussels sprouts	July 1–Aug. 15	Aug. 1–Sept. 1	Aug. 1–Sept. 15	Aug. 1–Oct. 1	Aug. 1–Nov. 1	Sept. 1–Dec. 31.
Cabbage [1]	Aug. 1–Sept. 1	Sept. 1–15	Sept. 1–Dec. 1	Sept. 1–Dec. 31	Sept. 1–Dec. 31	Sept. 1–Dec. 31.
Cabbage, Chinese	Aug. 1–Sept. 15	Aug. 15–Oct. 1	Sept. 1–Oct. 15	Sept. 1–Nov. 1	Sept. 1–Nov. 15	Sept. 1–Dec. 1.
Carrot	July 1–Aug. 15	Aug. 1–Sept. 1	Sept. 1–Nov. 1	Sept. 15–Dec. 1	Sept. 15–Dec. 1	Sept. 15–Dec. 1.
Cauliflower [1]	July 15–Aug. 15	Aug. 1–Sept. 1	Aug. 1–Sept. 15	Aug. 15–Oct. 10	Sept. 1–Oct. 20	Sept. 15–Nov. 1.
Celery [1] and celeriac	June 15–Aug. 15	July 1–Aug. 15	July 15–Sept. 1	Aug. 1–Dec. 1	Sept. 1–Dec. 31	Oct. 1–Dec. 31.
Chard	June 1–Sept. 10	June 1–Sept. 15	June 1–Oct. 1	June 1–Nov. 1	June 1–Dec. 1	June 1–Dec. 31.
Chervil and chives	(2)		Nov. 1–Dec. 31	Nov. 1–Dec. 31	Nov. 1–Dec. 31	Nov. 1–Dec. 31.
Chicory, witloof	July 1–Aug. 10	July 10–Aug. 20	July 20–Sept. 1	Aug. 15–Sept. 30	Aug. 15–Oct. 15	Aug. 15–Oct. 15.
Collards [1]	Aug. 1–Sept. 15	Aug. 15–Oct. 1	Aug. 25–Nov. 1	Sept. 1–Dec. 1	Sept. 1–Dec. 31	Sept. 1–Dec. 31.
Cornsalad	Sept. 15–Nov. 1	Oct. 1–Dec. 1	Oct. 1–Dec. 1	Oct. 1–Dec. 31	Oct. 1–Dec. 31	Oct. 1–Dec. 31.
Corn, sweet	June 1–Aug. 1	June 1–Aug. 15	June 1–Sept. 1			
Cress, upland	Sept. 15–Nov. 1	Oct. 1–Dec. 1	Oct. 1–Dec. 1	Oct. 1–Dec. 31	Oct. 1–Dec. 31	Oct. 1–Dec. 31.
Cucumber	June 1–Aug. 1	June 1–Aug. 15	June 1–Aug. 15	July 15–Sept. 15	Aug. 15–Oct. 1	Aug. 15–Oct. 1.
Eggplant [1]	June 1–July 1	June 1–July 15	June 1–Aug. 1	July 1–Sept. 1	Aug. 1–Sept. 30	Aug. 1–Sept. 30.
Endive	July 15–Aug. 15	Aug. 1–Sept. 1	Sept. 1–Oct. 1	Sept. 1–Nov. 15	Sept. 1–Dec. 1	Sept. 1–Dec. 1.
Fennel, Florence	July 1–Aug. 1	July 15–Aug. 15	Aug. 15–Sept. 15	Sept. 1–Nov. 15	Sept. 1–Dec. 1	Sept. 1–Dec. 1.
Garlic	(2)	Aug. 1–Oct. 1	Aug. 15–Oct. 1	Sept. 1–Nov. 15	Sept. 15–Nov. 15	Sept. 15–Nov. 15.
Horseradish [1]	(2)	(2)	(2)	(2)	(2)	(2)
Kale	July 15–Sept. 1	Aug. 1–Sept. 15	Aug. 15–Oct. 15	Sept. 1–Dec. 1	Sept. 1–Dec. 31	Sept. 1–Dec. 31.
Kohlrabi	Aug. 1–Sept. 1	Aug. 15–Sept. 15	Sept. 1–Oct. 15	Sept. 1–Dec. 1	Sept. 15–Dec. 31	Sept. 1–Dec. 31.
Leek	(2)	(2)	Sept. 1–Nov. 1	Sept. 1–Nov. 1	Sept. 1–Nov. 1	Sept. 15–Nov. 1
Lettuce, head [1]	Aug. 1–Sept. 15	Aug. 15–Oct. 15	Sept. 1–Nov. 1	Sept. 1–Dec. 1	Sept. 15–Dec. 31	Sept. 15–Dec. 31.
Lettuce, leaf	Aug. 15–Oct. 1	Aug. 25–Nov. 1	Sept. 1–Nov. 1	Sept. 1–Dec. 1	Sept. 15–Dec. 31	Sept. 15–Dec. 31.
Muskmelon	July 1–July 15	July 15–July 30				
Mustard	Aug. 15–Oct. 15	Aug. 15–Nov. 1	Sept. 1–Dec. 1	Sept. 1–Dec. 1	Sept. 1–Dec. 1	Sept. 15–Dec. 1.
Okra	June 1–Aug. 10	June 1–Aug. 20	June 1–Sept. 10	June 1–Sept. 20	Aug. 1–Oct. 1	Aug. 1–Oct. 1.
Onion [1]		Sept. 1–Oct. 15	Oct. 1–Dec. 31	Oct. 1–Dec. 31	Oct. 1–Dec. 31	Oct. 1–Dec. 31.
Onion, seed			Sept. 1–Nov. 1	Sept. 1–Nov. 1	Sept. 1–Nov. 1	Sept. 15–Nov. 1.
Onion, sets		Oct. 1–Dec. 1	Nov. 1–Dec. 31	Nov. 1–Dec. 31	Nov. 1–Dec. 31	Nov. 1–Dec. 31.
Parsley	Aug. 1–Sept. 15	Sept. 1–Nov. 15	Sept. 1–Dec. 31	Sept. 1–Dec. 31	Sept. 1–Dec. 31	Sept. 1–Dec. 1.
Parsnip	(2)	(2)	Aug. 1–Sept. 1	Sept. 1–Nov. 15	Sept. 1–Dec. 1	Sept. 1–Dec. 1.
Peas, garden	Aug. 1–Sept. 15	Sept. 1–Nov. 1	Oct. 1–Dec. 1	Oct. 1–Dec. 31	Oct. 1–Dec. 31	Oct. 1–Dec. 31.
Peas, black-eye	June 1–Aug. 1	June 15–Aug. 15	July 1–Sept. 1	July 1–Sept. 10	July 1–Sept. 20	July 1–Sept. 20.
Pepper [1]	June 1–July 20	June 1–Aug. 1	June 1–Aug. 15	June 15–Sept. 1	Aug. 15–Oct. 1	Aug. 1–Sept. 15.
Potato	July 20–Aug. 10	July 25–Aug. 20	Aug. 10–Sept. 15	Aug. 1–Sept. 15	Aug. 1–Sept. 15	Aug. 1–Sept. 15.
Radish	Aug. 15–Oct. 15	Sept. 1–Nov. 15	Sept. 1–Dec. 1	Sept. 1–Dec. 31	Aug. 1–Sept. 15	Oct. 1–Dec. 31.
Rhubarb [1]	Nov. 1–Dec. 1					
Rutabaga	July 15–Aug. 1	July 15–Aug. 15	Aug. 1–Sept. 1	Sept. 1–Nov. 15	Oct. 1–Nov. 15	Oct. 15–Nov. 15.
Salsify	June 1–July 10	June 15–July 20	July 15–Aug. 15	Aug. 15–Sept. 30	Aug. 15–Oct. 15	Sept. 1–Oct. 31.
Shallot	(2)	Aug. 1–Oct. 1	Aug. 15–Oct. 1	Aug. 15–Oct. 15	Sept. 15–Nov. 1	Sept. 15–Nov. 1.
Sorrel	Aug. 1–Sept. 15	Aug. 15–Oct. 1	Aug. 15–Oct. 15	Sept. 1–Nov. 15	Sept. 1–Dec. 15	Sept. 1–Dec. 31.
Soybean	June 1–July 15	June 1–July 25	June 1–July 30	June 1–July 30	June 1–July 30	June 1–July 30.
Spinach	Sept. 1–Oct. 1	Sept. 15–Nov. 1	Oct. 1–Dec. 1	Oct. 1–Dec. 31	Oct. 1–Dec. 31	Oct. 1–Dec. 31.
Spinach, New Zealand	June 1–Aug. 1	June 1–Aug. 15	June 1–Aug. 15			
Squash, summer	June 1–Aug. 1	June 1–Aug. 10	June 1–Aug. 20	June 1–Sept. 1	June 1–Sept. 15	June 1–Oct. 1.
Squash, winter	June 10–July 10	June 20–July 20	July 1–Aug. 1	July 15–Aug. 15	Aug. 1–Sept. 1	Aug. 1–Sept. 1.
Sweetpotato	June 1–15	June 1–July 1	June 1–July 1	June 1–July 1	June 1–July 1	June 1–July 1.
Tomato	June 1–July 1	June 1–July 15	June 1–Aug. 1	Aug. 1–Sept. 1	Aug. 15–Oct. 1	Sept. 1–Nov. 1.
Turnip	Aug. 1–Sept. 15	Sept. 1–Oct. 15	Sept. 1–Nov. 15	Sept. 1–Nov. 15	Oct. 1–Dec. 1	Oct. 1–Dec. 31.
Watermelon	July 1–July 15	July 15–July 30				

[1] Plants.
[2] Generally spring-planted (table 4).

21

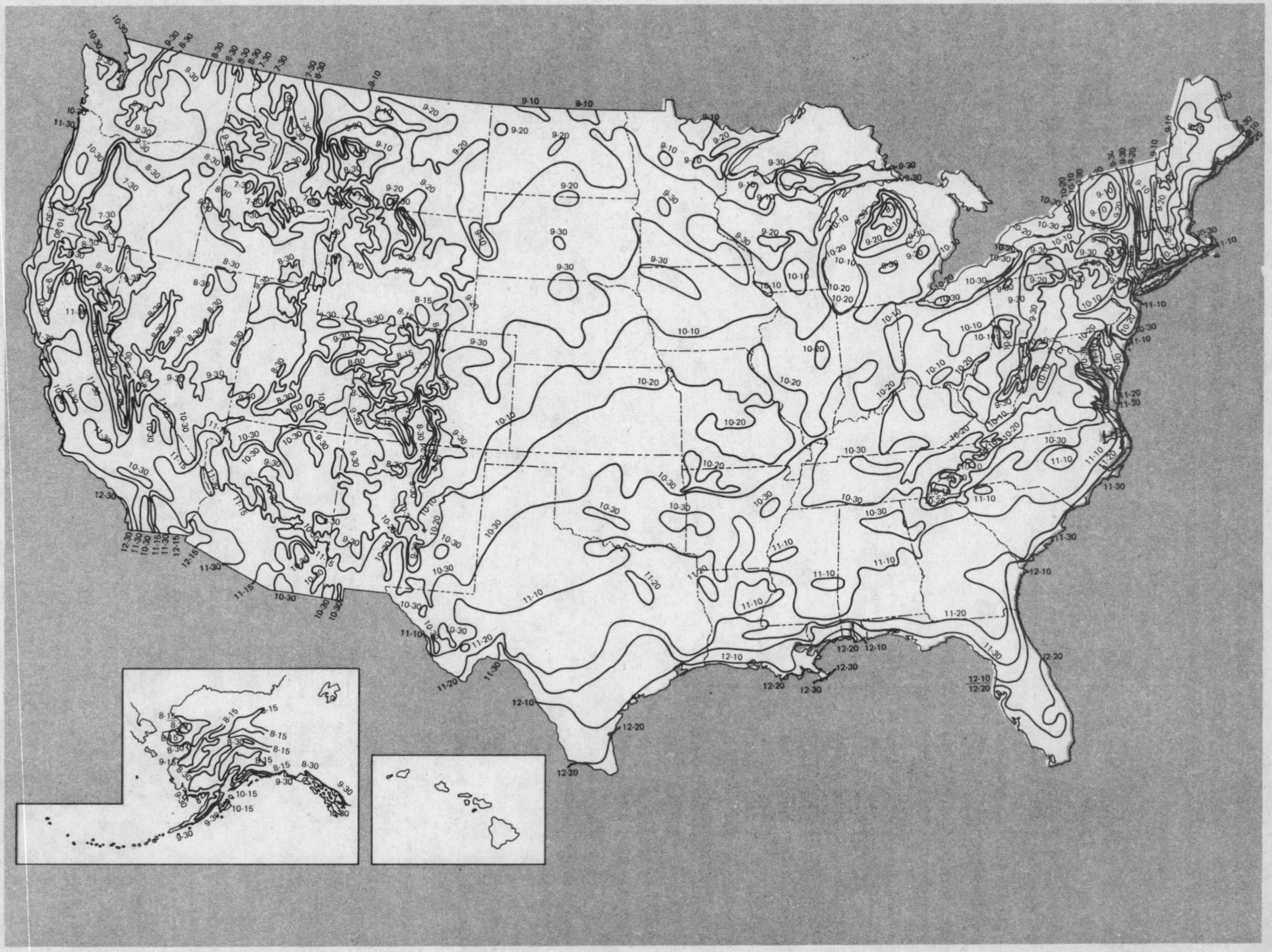

Figure 13.—Average dates of the first killing frost in fall.

It is much better to give the garden a good soaking about once a week than to water it sparingly more often. Light sprinklings at frequent intervals do little, if any, good. The best way to apply water, when the soil and slope are suitable, is to run it the length of furrows between the rows until the soil is well soaked. If the soil is very sandy or the surface too irregular for the furrow method, sprinklers or porous irrigaing hose must be used.

Controlling Weeds

Weeds rob cultivated plants of water, nutrients, and light. Some weeds harbor diseases, insects, and nematodes that reinfest garden crops in succeeding years.

As soon as the soil can be properly worked after each rain or irrigation, it should be thoroughly hoed or cultivated to kill weeds that have sprouted and to leave the surface in a loose, friable condition to absorb later rainfall. The primary value of hoeing or cultivating is weed control. This cultivation should be shallow so as to avoid injuring the vegetable plant roots that lie near the surface. Although it is desirable to keep the surface soil loose, there is little to be gained by hoeing or cultivating oftener than necessary to keep weeds out of the garden.

In small gardens, weeds can be controlled with black polyethylene mulch (fig. 14) supplemented by hand weeding such as pulling, hoeing, and wheel hoeing. Mulching vegetable crops with organic material also is a common practice in small gardens.

The best organic mulches are partially decomposed hay, straw, or grass clippings. The mulch should be applied 4 to 6 inches deep when the plants are about 6 inches tall. Cabbage, tomato, and other transplants usually are tall enough soon after they are set in the garden. Before applying mulch, hoe out all small weeds. Not only does mulch control weeds, it also conserves moisture, keeps the soil from packing, and increases the humus necessary for vigorous plant growth.

Controlling Diseases and Insects

Garden crops are subject to attack by a number of diseases and insects. Preventive measures are best, but if an attack occurs and the gardener is not familiar with the insect or disease and the proper treatment to protect his crop, he is advised to consult the county agent or write immediately to his experiment station. The

Among the most important disease-control measures are the use of disease-free seeds and plants, and the use of disease-resistant varieties. Great progress has been made within recent years in the development of varieties that are resistant to certain diseases.

Figure 14.—Black plastic film conserves moisture, controls weeds, warms the soil, and hastens maturity of vegetable crops.

Growing Specific Vegetables

Perennial Vegetables

The larger vegetables gardens need a number of perennials. Asparagus, horseradish, and rhubarb are the most important, but chives, bottom multiplier onions, and some of the flavoring and condiment plants, chiefly sage and mint, are also desirable. Unfortunately, asparagus, horseradish, and rhubarb are not adapted to conditions in the lower South.

All the perennial crops should be grouped together along one side of the garden, where they will not interfere with work on the annual crops.

Asparagus

Asparagus is among the earliest of spring vegetables. An area about 20 feet square, or a row 50 to 75 feet long, will supply plenty of fresh asparagus for a family of five or six persons, provided the soil is well enriched and the plants are given good attention. More must be planted if a supply is to be canned or frozen.

Asparagus does best where winters are cold enough to freeze the ground to a depth of a few inches at least. In many southern areas the plants make a weak growth, producing small shoots. Elevation has some effect, but, in general, the latitude of south-central Georgia is the southern limit of profitable culture.

The crop can be grown on almost any well-drained, fertile soil, and there is little possibility of having the soil too rich, especially through the use of manure. Loosen the soil far down, either by subsoil plowing or by deep spading before planting. Throw the topsoil aside and spade manure, leafmold, rotted leaves, or peat into the subsoil to a depth of 14 to 16 inches; then mix from 5 to 10 pounds of a complete fertilizer into each 75-foot row or 20-foot bed.

When the soil is ready for planting, the bottom of the trench should be about 6 inches below the natural level of the soil. After the crowns are set and covered to a depth of an inch or two, gradually work the soil into the trench around the plants during the first season. When set in beds, asparagus plants should be at least 1½ feet apart each way; when set in rows, they should be about 1½ feet apart with the rows from 4 to 5 feet apart.

Asparagus plants, or crowns, are grown from seed. The use of 1-year-old plants only is recommended. These should have a root spread of at least 15 inches, and larger ones are better. The home gardener will usually find it best to buy his plants from a grower who has a good strain of a recognized variety. Mary Washington and Waltham Washington are good varieties that have the added merit of being rust resistant. Waltham Washington is an improved strain of Mary Washington. It contains very little of the purple over-cast predominant in the Mary Washington, is a high yielder, and has good green color clear into the ground line. In procuring asparagus crowns, it is always well to be sure that they have not been allowed to dry out.

Clean cultivation encourages vigorous growth; it behooves the gardener to keep his asparagus clean from the start. In a large farm garden, with long rows, most of the work can be done with a horse-drawn cultivator or a garden tractor. In a small garden, where the rows are short or the asparagus is planted in beds, however, hand work is necessary.

For a 75-foot row, an application of manure and 6 to 8 pounds of a high-grade complete fertilizer, once each year, is recommended. Manure and fertilizer may be applied either before or after the cutting season.

Remove no shoots the year the plants are set in the permanent bed and keep the cutting period short the year after setting. Remove all shoots during the cutting season in subsequent years (fig. 15). Cease cutting about July 1 to 10 and let the tops grow. In the autumn, remove and burn the dead tops.

Asparagus rust and asparagus beetles are the chief enemies of the crop.

Figure 15.—Asparagus shoots ready to be cut.

Horseradish

Horseradish is adapted to the north-temperate regions of the United States, but not to the South, except possibly in the high altitudes.

Any good soil, except possibly the lightest sands and heaviest clays, will grow horseradish, but it does best on a deep, rich, moist loam that is well supplied with organic matter. Avoid shallow soil; it produces rough, prongy roots. Mix organic matter with the soil a few months before the plants or cuttings are set. Some fertilizer may be used at the time of planting and more during the subsequent seasons. A top dressing of organic matter each spring is advisable.

Horseradish is propagated either by crowns or by root cuttings. In propagating by crowns a portion of an old plant consisting of a piece of root and crown buds is merely lifted and planted in a new place. Root cuttings are pieces of older roots 6 to 8 inches long and of the thickness of a lead pencil. They may be saved when preparing the larger roots for grating, or they may be purchased from seedsmen. A trench 4 or 5 inches deep is opened with a hoe and the root cuttings are placed at an angle with their tops near the surface of the ground. Plants from these cuttings usually make good roots the first year. As a rule, the plants in the home garden are allowed to grow from year to year, and portions of the roots are removed as needed. Pieces of roots and crowns remaining in the soil are usually sufficient to reestablish the plants.

There is very little choice in the matter of varieties of horseradish. Be sure, however, to obtain good healthy planting stock of a strain that is giving good results in the area where it is being grown. New Bohemian is perhaps the best known sort sold by American seedsmen.

Rhubarb

Rhubarb thrives best in regions having cool moist summers and winters cold enough to freeze the ground to a depth of several inches. It is not adapted to most parts of the South, but in certain areas of higher elevation it does fairly well. A few hills along the garden fence will supply all that a family can use.

Any deep, well-drained, fertile soil is suitable for rhubarb. Spade the soil or plow it to a depth of 12 to 16 inches and mix in rotted manure, leafmold, decayed hardwood leaves, sods, or other form of organic matter. The methods of soil preparation suggested for asparagus are suitable for rhubarb. As rhubarb is planted in hills 3 to 4 feet apart, however, it is usually sufficient to prepare each hill separately.

Rhubarb plants may be started from seed and transplanted, but seedlings vary from the parent plant. The usual method of starting the plants is to obtain pieces of crowns from established hills and set them in prepared hills. Top-dress the planting with a heavy application of organic matter in either early spring or late fall. Organic matter applied over the hills during early spring greatly hastens growth, or forces the plant.

A pound of complete commercial fertilizer high in nitrogen applied around each hill every year insures an abundant supply of plant food. The plants can be mulched with green grass or weeds.

Remove seedstalks as soon as they form. No leaf stems should be harvested before the second year and but few until the third. Moreover, the harvest season must be largely confined to early spring. The hills should be divided and reset every 7 or 8 years. Otherwise, they become too thick and produce only slender stems.

Crimson, Red Valentine, MacDonald, Canada Red, and Victoria are standard varieties.

Use only the leafstalk as a food. **Rhubarb leaves contain injurious substances, including oxalic acid. Never use them for food.**

Sorrel

Sorrel is a perennial that is usually started from seeds. It requires a rich, mellow, well-drained soil. Rows may be of any convenient distance apart. Thin the plants to about 8 inches apart in the rows. If the leaves alone are gathered and the plants are cultivated to prevent the growth of weeds, a planting should last 3 or 4 years. French Broad Leaf is a well-known variety.

Greens

Greens are usually the leaves and leaf stems of immature plants, which in their green state are boiled for food. Young, tender branches of certain plants, New Zealand spinach, for example, are also used this way. All the plants treated here as greens except New Zealand spinach are hardy vegetables, most of them adapted to fall sowing and winter culture over the entire South and in the more temperate parts of the North. Their culture may be extended more widely in the North by growing them with some protection, such as mulching or frames.

Chard

Chard, or Swiss chard (fig. 16), is a type of beet that has been developed for its tops instead of its roots. Crop after crop of the outer leaves may be harvested without injuring the plant. Only one planting is necessary, and a row 30 to 40 feet long will supply a family for the entire summer. Each seed cluster contains several seeds, and fairly wide spacing of the seeds facilitates thinning. The culture of chard is practically the same as that of beets, but the plants grow larger and need to be thinned to at least 6 inches apart in the row. Chard needs a rich, mellow soil, and it is sensitive to soil acidity.

Witloof Chicory

Witloof chicory, or French endive, is grown for both roots and tops. It is a hardy plant, not especially sensitive to heat or cold. It does, however, need a deep, rich, loamy soil without too much organic matter. The tops are sometimes harvested while young. The roots are lifted in

Figure 16.—Swiss chard is especially suitable for hot-weather culture.

autumn and placed in a box or bed of moist soil in a warm cellar for forcing. They must be covered with a few inches of sand. Under this covering the leaves form in a solid head, known on the market as witloof.

The culture of chicory is simple. Sow the seeds in spring or early summer in drills about 18 inches apart. Later, thin the plants to 6 or 8 inches apart in the rows. If sown too early the plants shoot to seed and are worthless for forcing. The kind known as witloof is most generally used.

Collards

Collards are grown and used about like cabbage. They withstand heat better than other members of the cabbage group, and are well liked in the South for both summer and winter use. Collards do not form a true head, but a large rosette of leaves, which may be blanched by tying together.

Cornsalad

Cornsalad is also known as lamb's-lettuce and fetticus. Sow the seed in early spring in drills and cultivate the plants the same as lettuce or mustard. For an extra early crop, plant the seed in the autumn and cover the plants lightly through the winter. In the Southern States the covering is not necessary, and the plants are ready for use in February and March. The leaves are frequently used in their natural green state, but they may be blanched by covering the rows with anything that will exclude light.

Kale

Kale, or borecole, is hardy and lives over winter in latitudes as far north as northern Maryland and southern Pennsylvania and in other areas where similar winter conditions prevail. It is also resistant to heat and may be grown in summer. Its real merit, however, is a cool-weather greens.

Kale is a member of the cabbage family. The best garden varieties are low-growing, spreading plants, with thick, more or less crinkled leaves (fig. 17). Vates Blue Curled, Dwarf Blue Scotch, and Siberian are well-known garden varieties.

No other plant is so well adapted to fall sowing throughout a wide area of both North and South or in areas characterized by winters of moderate severity. Kale may well follow some such early-season vegetable as green beans, potatoes, or peas.

In the autumn the seed may be broadcast very thinly and then lightly raked into the soil. Except for spring sowings, made when weeds are troublesome, sow kale in rows 18 to 24 inches apart and later thin the plants to about a foot apart.

Kale may be harvested either by cutting the entire plant or by taking the larger leaves while young. Old kale is tough and stringy.

Mustard

Mustard grows well on almost any good soil. As the plants require but a short time to reach the proper stage for use, frequent sowings are recommended. Sow the seeds thickly in drills as early as possible in the spring or, for late use, in September or October. The forms of Indian mustard, the leaves of which are often curled and frilled, are generally used. Southern Curled and Green Wave are common sorts.

Spinach

Spinach is a hardy cool-weather plant that withstands winter conditions in the South. In most of the North, spinach is primarily an early-spring and late-fall crop, but in some areas, where summer temperatures are mild, it may be grown continuously from early spring until late fall. It should be emphasized that summer and winter culture of spinach is possible only where moderate temperatures prevail.

Spinach will grow on almost any well-drained, fertile soil where sufficient moisture is available. It is very sensitive to acid soil. If a soil test shows the need, apply lime to the part of the garden used for spinach, regardless of the treatment given the rest of the area.

The application of 100 pounds of rotted manure and 3 to 4 pounds of commercial fertilizer to each 100 square feet of land is suitable for spinach in the home garden. Broadcast both manure and fertilizer and work them in before sowing the seed.

Long Standing Bloomsdale is perhaps the most popular variety seeded in spring. It is attractive, grows quickly, is very productive, and will stand for a moderate length of time before going to seed. Virginia Savoy and Hybrid No. 7 are valuable varieties for fall planting, as they are resistant to yellows, or blight. Hybrid No. 7 is also resistant to downy mildew (blue mold). These two varieties are very cold-hardy but are not suitable for the spring crop, as they produce seedstalks too early. For horse or tractor cultivation, the rows of the garden should be not less than 24 inches apart; when land is plentiful they may be 30 inches apart. For wheel-hoe or hand work, the rows should be 14 to 16 inches apart. Spinach may be drilled by hand in furrows about 1 inch deep and covered with fine earth not more than ½ inch deep, or it may be drilled with a seed drill, which distributes the seed more evenly than is ordi-

Figure 17.—Kale, a hardy green, is mulched here with spoiled hay.

narily possible by hand. Thin the plants to 3 or 4 inches apart before they crowd in the row.

New Zealand Spinach

New Zealand spinach is not related to common spinach. It is a large plant, with thick, succulent leaves and stems, and grows with a branching, spreading habit to a height of 2 or more feet. It thrives in hot weather and is grown as a substitute in seasons when ordinary spinach cannot withstand the heat. New Zealand spinach thrives on soils suitable for common spinach. Because of their larger size, these plants must have more room. The rows should be at least 3 feet apart, with the plants about 1½ feet apart in the rows. As prompt germination may be difficult, the seeds should be soaked for 1 or 2 hours in water at 120° F. before being planted. They may be sown, 1 to 1½ inches deep, as soon as danger of frost is past. Successive harvests of the tips may be made from a single planting, as new leaves and branches are readily produced. Care must be taken not to remove too large a portion of the plant at one time.

Turnip Greens

Varieties of turnips usually grown for the roots are also planted for the greens. Shogoin is a favorable variety for greens. It is resistant to aphid damage and produces fine-quality white roots if allowed to grow. Seven Top is a leafy sort that produces no edible root. As a rule, sow turnips to be used for greens thickly and then thin them, leaving all but the greens to develop as a root crop. Turnip greens are especially adapted to winter and early-spring culture in the South. The cultural methods employed are the same as those for turnip and rutabaga.

Salad Vegetables

The group known as salad crops includes vegetables that are usually eaten raw with salt, pepper, vinegar, and salad oil, or with mayonnaise or other dressings. This classification is entirely one of convenience; some vegetables not included in this group are used in the same way. Some members of this class may be cooked and used as greens.

Celery

Celery can be grown in home gardens in most parts of the country at some time during the year. It is a cool-weather crop and adapted to winter culture in the lower South. In the upper South and in the North it may be grown either as an early-spring or as a late-fall crop. Farther north in certain favored locations it can be grown throughout the summer.

Rich, moist but well-drained, deeply prepared, mellow soil is essential for celery. Soil varying from sand to clay loam and to peat may be used as long as these requirements are met. Unless the ground is very fertile, plenty of organic material, supplemented by liberal applications of commercial fertilizer, is necessary. For a 100-foot row of celery, 5 pounds of a high-grade complete fertilizer thoroughly mixed with the soil are none too much. Prepare the celery row a week or two before setting the plants.

The most common mistake with celery is failure to allow enough time for growing the plants. About 10 weeks are needed to grow good celery plants. Celery seed is small and germinates slowly. A good method is to place the seeds in a muslin bag and soak them overnight, then mix them with dry sand, distribute them in shallow trenches in the seed flats or seedbed, and cover them with leafmold or similar material to a depth of not more than ½ inch. Keep the bed covered with moist burlap sacks. Celery plants are very delicate and must be kept free from weeds. They are made more stocky by being transplanted once before they are set in the garden, but this practice retards their growth. When they are to be transplanted before being set in the ground, the rows in the seed box or seedbed may be only a few inches apart. When they are to remain in the box until transplanted to the garden, however, the plants should be about 2 inches apart each way. In beds, the rows should be 10 to 12 inches apart, with seedlings 1 to 1½ inches apart in the row.

For hand culture celery plants are set in rows 18 to 24 inches apart; for tractor cultivation 30 to 36 inches apart. The plants are spaced about 6 inches in the row. Double rows are about a foot apart. Set celery on a cool or cloudy day, if possible; and if the soil is at all dry, water the plants thoroughly. If the plants are large, it is best to pinch off the outer leaves 3 or 4 inches from the base before setting. In bright weather it is well also to shade the plants for a day or two after they are set. Small branches bearing green leaves, stuck in the ground, protect the plants from intense sun without excluding air. As soon as the plants attain some size, gradually work the soil around them to keep them upright. Be careful to get no soil into the hearts of the plants. Early celery is blanched by excluding the light with boards, paper, drain tiles, or other devices. Late celery may be blanched also by banking with earth or by storing in the dark. Banking celery with soil in warm weather causes it to decay.

Late celery may be kept for early-winter use by banking with earth and covering the tops with leaves or straw to keep them from freezing, or it may be dug and stored in a cellar or a coldframe, with the roots well embedded in moist soil. While in storage it must be kept as cool as possible without freezing.

For the home garden Golden Detroit, Summer Pascal (Waltham Improved), and the Golden Plume are adapted for the early crop to be used during late summer, fall, and early winter. For storage and for use after the holiday season, it is desirable to plant some such variety as Green Light or Utah 52–70.

Endive

Endive closely resembles lettuce in its requirements, except that it is less sensitive to heat. It may be substituted for lettuce when the culture of lettuce is impracticable. In the South, it is mainly a winter crop. In the North, it is grown in spring, summer, and autumn and is also forced in winter. Full Heart Batavian and Salad King are good varieties. Broadleaved endive is known on the markets as escarole.

Cultural details are the same as those for head lettuce. When the plants are large and well-formed, draw the leaves together and tie them so that the heart will blanch. For winter use, lift the plants with a ball of earth, place them in a cellar or coldframe where they will not freeze, and tie and blanch them as needed.

Lettuce

Lettuce can be grown in any home garden. It is a cool-weather crop, being as sensitive to heat as any vegetable grown. In the South, lettuce culture is confined to late fall, winter, and spring. In colder parts of the South, lettuce may not live through the winter. In the North, lettuce culture is particially limited to spring and autumn. In some favored locations, such as areas of high altitude or in far-northern latitudes, lettuce grows to perfection in summer. Planting at a wrong season is responsible for most of the failures with this crop.

Any rich soil is adapted to lettuce, although the plant is sensitive to acid soil. A commercial fertilizer with a heavy proportion of phosphorus is recommended.

Start spring lettuce indoors or in a hotbed and transplant it to the garden when the plants have four of five leaves. Gardeners need not wait for the end of light frosts, as lettuce is not usually harmed by a temperature as low as 28° F., if the plants have been properly hardened. Allow about 6 weeks for growing the plants. For the fall crop the seed may be sown directly in the row and thinned; there is no gain in transplanting.

For tractor cultivation, set lettuce plants 12 to 15 inches apart in rows 30 to 36 inches apart; for hand culture, about 14 to 16 inches apart each way. Where gardeners grow leaf lettuce or desire merely the leaves and not well-developed heads, the spacing in the rows may be much closer. In any case it is usually best to cut the entire plant instead of removing the leaves.

There are many excellent varieties of lettuce, all of which do well in the garden when conditions are right. Of the loose-leaf kinds, Black-Seeded Simpson, Grand Rapids, Slobolt, and Saladbowl (fig. 18) are among the best. Saladbowl and Slobolt are heat resistant and very desirable for warm-weather culture. Of the heading sorts, Buttercrunch, White Boston, Fulton, and Great Lakes are among the best. The White Boston requires less time than the three others. Where warm weather comes early, it is seldom worth while to sow head lettuce seed in the open ground in the spring with the expectation of obtaining firm heads.

Parsley

Parsley is hardy to cold but sensitive to heat. It thrives under much the same temperature

29

Figure 18.—Saladbowl lettuce is an outstanding leaf lettuce with considerable heat resistance.

conditions as kale, lettuce, and spinach. If given a little protection it may be carried over winter through most of the North.

Parsley thrives on any good soil. As the plant is delicate during its early stages of growth, however, the land should be mellow.

Parsley seeds are small and germinate slowly. Soaking in water overnight hastens the germination. In the North, it is a good plan to sow the seeds indoors and transplant the plants to the garden, thereby getting a crop before hot weather. In the South, it is usually possible to sow the seed directly in drills. For the fall crop in the North, row seeding is also practiced. After seeding, it is well to lay a board over the row for a few days until the first seedlings appear. After its removal day-to-day watering will insure germination of as many seeds as possible. Parsley rows should be 14 to 16 inches apart, with the plants 4 to 6 inches apart in the rows. A few feet will supply the family, and a few plants transplanted to the coldframe in the autumn will give a supply during early spring.

Upland Cress

Upland cress, sometimes erroneously called peppergrass, is a hardy plant. It may be sown in all the milder parts of the country in autumn. In the colder sections it is sown in early spring as soon as the ground can be worked. The seeds are small and must not be covered deeply. After the plants are well established, thin them to 4 to 6 inches apart in the rows. This is a short-season crop that should

be planted in quick succession to insure a steady supply.

Root Vegetables

Potatoes in the North and sweetpotatoes in the South are grown in almost every garden. Beets, carrots, and turnips are also widely grown in gardens. The vegetables in this group may be used throughout the growing season and also be kept for winter.

Beet

The beet is well adapted to all parts of the country. It is fairly tolerant of heat; it is also resistant to cold. However, it will not withstand severe freezing. In the Northern States, where winters are too severe, the beet is grown in spring, summer, and autumn.

Beets are sensitive to strongly acid soils, and it is wise to apply lime if a test shows the need for it. Good beet quality depends on quick growth; for this the land must be fertile, well-drained, and in good physical condition.

Midsummer heat and drought may interfere with seed germination. By covering the seeds with sandy soil, leafmold, or other material that will not bake and by keeping the soil damp until the plants are up, much of this trouble can be avoided. Make successive sowings at intervals of about 3 weeks in order to have a continuous supply of young, tender beets throughout the season.

Where cultivating is by hand, the rows may be about 16 inches apart; where it is by tractor, they must be wider. Beet seed as purchased consists of small balls, each containing several seeds. On most soils the seed should be covered to a depth of about an inch. After the plants are well established, thin them to stand 2 to 3 inches apart in the rows.

Early Wonder, Crosby Egyptian, and Detroit Dark Red are standard varieties suitable for early home-garden planting, while Long Season remains tender and edible over a long season.

Carrot

Carrots are usually grown in the fall, winter, and spring in the South, providing an almost continuous supply. In the North, carrots can be grown and used through the summer and the surplus stored for winter. Carrots will grow on almost any type of soil as long as it is moist, fertile, loose, and free from clods and stones, but sandy loams and peats are best. Use commercial fertilizer.

Because of their hardiness, carrots may be seeded as early in the spring as the ground can be worked. Succession plantings at intervals of 3 weeks will insure a continuous supply of tender carrots. Cover carrot seed about ½ inch on most soils; less, usually about ¼ inch, on heavy soils. With care in seeding, little thinning is necessary; carrots can stand some crowding, especially on loose soils. However, they should be no thicker than 10 to 15 plants per foot of row.

Chantenay, Nantes, and Imperator are standard sorts. Carrots should be stored before hard frosts occur, as the roots may be injured by cold.

Celeriac

Celeriac, or turnip-rooted celery, has been developed for the root instead of the top. Its culture is the same as that of celery, and the enlarged roots can be used at any time after they are big enough. The late-summer crop of celeriac may be stored for winter use. In areas having mild winters the roots may be left in the ground and covered with a mulch of several inches of straw or leaves, or they may be lifted, packed in moist sand, and stored in a cool cellar.

Chervil

Chervil comes in two distinct types, salad chervil and turnip-rooted chervil. Salad chervil is grown about like parsley. The seeds must be bedded in damp sand for a few weeks before being sown; otherwise, their germination is very slow.

Turnip-rooted chervil thrives in practically all parts of the country where the soil is fertile and the moisture sufficient. In the South, the seeds are usually sown in the fall, but they may not germinate until spring. In the North, the seeds may be sown in the autumn to germinate in the spring; or the plants may be started indoors in later winter and transplanted to open ground later on. The spacing and culture of chervil are about the same as for beets and carrots.

Dasheen

The dasheen, a large-growing plant, is related to the ordinary elephant's-ear and looks like it. It is a long-season crop, adapted for culture only in the South, where there is normally a very warm frostless season of at least 7 months. It needs a rich loamy soil, an abundance of moisture with good drainage, and a fairly moist atmosphere. Small tubers—from 2 to 5 ounces in weight—are used for planting in much the same way as potatoes. Planting may be done 2 or 3 weeks before frosts are over, and the season may be lengthened by starting the plants indoors and setting them out after frost is past. Set the plants in 3½- to 4-foot rows, about 2 feet apart in the rows. Dasheen tubers may be dug and dried on the ground in much the same way as sweetpotatoes, and stored at 50° F. with ventilation.

Parsnip

The parsnip is adapted to culture over a wide portion of the United States. It must have warm soil and weather at planting time, but does not thrive in midsummer in the South.

In many parts of the South parsnips are grown and used during early summer. They should not reach maturity during midsummer, however. Furthermore, it is difficult to obtain good germination in the summer, which limits their culture during the autumn.

Any deep, fertile soil will grow parsnips, but light, friable soil, with no tendency to bake, is best. Stony or lumpy soils are objectionable; they may cause rough, prongy roots.

Parsnip seed must be fresh—not more than a year old–and it is well to sow rather thickly and thin to about 3 inches apart. Parsnips germinate slowly, but it is possible to hasten germination by covering the seed with leafmold, sand, a mixture of sifted coal ashes and soil, peat, or some similar material that will not bake. Rolling a light soil over the row or trampling it firmly after seeding usually hastens and improves germination. Hollow Crown and All American are suitable varieties.

Parsnips may be dug and stored in a cellar or pit or left in the ground until used. Roots placed in cold storage gain in quality faster than those left in the ground, and freezing in the ground in winter improves the quality.

31

There is no basis for the belief that parsnips that remain in the ground over winter and start growth in the spring are poisonous. All reported cases of poisoning from eating so-called wild parsnips have been traced to water hemlock (*Cicuta*), which belongs to the same family and resembles the parsnip somewhat.

Be very careful in gathering wild plants that look like the parsnip.

Potato

Potatoes, when grown under favorable conditions, are one of the most productive of all vegetables in terms of food per unit area of land.

Potatoes are a cool-season crop; they do not thrive in midsummer in the southern half of the country. Any mellow, fertile, well-drained soil is suitable for potato production. Stiff, heavy clay soils often produce misshapen tubers. Potatoes respond to a generous use of commercial fertilizer, but if the soil is too heavily limed, the tubers may be scabby.

Commercial 5–8–5 or 5–8–7 mixtures applied at 1,000 to 2,000 pounds to the acre (approximately 7½ to 15 pounds to each 100-foot row) usually provide enough plant food for a heavy crop. The lower rate of application is sufficient for very fertile soils; the higher rate for less fertile ones. Commercial fertilizer can be applied at the time of planting, but it should be mixed with the soil in such a way that the seed pieces will not come in direct contact with it.

In the North, plant two types of potatoes— one to provide early potatoes for summer use, the other for storage and winter use. Early varieties include Irish Cobbler, Early Gem, Norland, Norgold Russet, and Superior. Best late varieties are Katahdin, Kennebec, Chippewa, Russet Burbank, Sebago, and the golden nemotode resistant Wanseon. Irish Cobbler is the most widely adapted of the early varieties and Katahdin of the late. In the Great Plains States, Pontiac and Red La Soda are preferred for summer use; the Katahdin and Russet Burbank for winter. In the Pacific Northwest, the Russet Burbank, White Rose, Kennebec, and Early Gem are used. In the Southern States, the Irish Cobbler, Red La Soda, Red Pontiac, and Pungo are widely

grown. The use of certified seed is always advisable.

In preparing seed potatoes for planting, cut them into blocky rather than wedge-shaped pieces. Each piece should be about 1½ ounces in weight and have at least one eye. Medium-sized tubers weighing 5 to 7 ounces are cut to best advantage.

Plant early potatoes as soon as weather and soil conditions permit. Fall preparation of the soil often makes it possible to plant the early crop without delay in late winter or early spring. Potatoes require 2 to 3 weeks to come up, depending on depth of planting and the temperature of the soil. In some sections the ground may freeze slightly, but this is seldom harmful unless the sprouts have emerged. Prolonged cold and wet weather after planting is likely to cause the seed pieces to rot. Hence, avoid too early planting. Young potato plants are often damaged by frost, but they usually renew their growth quickly from uninjured portions of the stems.

Do not dig potatoes intended for storage until the tops are mature. Careful handling to avoid skinning is desirable, and protection from long exposure to light is necessary to prevent their becoming green and unfit for table use. Store in a well-ventilated place where the temperature is low, 45° to 50° if possible, but where there is no danger of freezing.

Radish

Radishes are hardy to cold, but they cannot withstand heat. In the South, they do well in autumn, winter, and spring. In the North, they may be grown in spring and autumn, and in sections having mild winters they may be grown in coldframes at that season. In high altitudes and in northern locations with cool summers, radishes thrive from early spring to late autumn.

Radishes are not sensitive to the type of soil so long as it is rich, moist, and friable. Apply additional fertilizer when the seeds are sown; conditions must be favorable for quick growth. Radishes that grow slowly have a pungent flavor and are undesirable.

Radishes mature the quickest of our garden crops. They remain in prime condition only a few days, which makes small plantings at week or 10-day intervals advisable. A few yards of row will supply all the radishes a family will consume during the time the radishes are at their best.

There are two types of radishes—the mild, small, quick-maturing sorts such as Scarlet Globe, French Breakfast, and Cherry Belle, all of which reach edible size in from 20 to 40 days; and the more pungent, large, winter radishes such as Long Black Spanish and China Rose, which require 75 days or more for growth. Plant winter radishes so they will reach a desirable size in the autumn. Gather and store them like other root crops.

Salsify

Salsify, or vegetable oyster, may be grown in practically all parts of the country. It is similar to parsnips in its requirements but needs a slightly longer growing season. For this reason it cannot be grown as far north as parsnips. Salsify, however, is somewhat more hardy and can be sown earlier in the spring.

Thoroughly prepare soil for salsify to a depth of at least a foot. Lighten heavy garden soil by adding sand or comparable material. Salsify must have plenty of plant food.

Sandwich Island is the best-known variety. A half ounce of seed will sow a 50-foot row, enough for most families. Always use fresh seed; salsify seed retains its vitality only 1 year.

Salsify may be left in the ground over winter or lifted and stored like parsnips or other root crops.

Sweetpotato

Sweetpotatoes succeed best in the South, but they are grown in home gardens as far north as southern New York and southern Michigan. They can be grown even farther north, in sections having especially mild climates, such as the Pacific Northwest. In general, sweetpotatoes may be grown wherever there is a frost-free period of about 150 days with relatively high temperature. Jersey Orange, Nugget, and Nemagold are the commonest dry-fleshed varieties; Centennial, Porto Rico, and Goldrush are three of the best of the moist type.

A well-drained, moderately deep sandy loam of medium fertility is best for sweetpotatoes.

Heavy clays and very deep loose-textured soils encourage the formation of long stringy roots. For best results the soil should be moderately fertilized throughout. If applied under the rows, the fertilizer should be well mixed with the soil.

In most of the area over which sweetpotatoes are grown it is necessary to start the plants in a hotbed, because the season is too short to produce a good crop after the weather warms enough to start plants outdoors. Bed roots used for seed close together in a hotbed and cover them with about 2 inches of sand or fine soil, such as leafmold. It is not safe to set the plants in the open ground until the soil is warm and the weather settled. Toward the last, ventilate the hotbed freely to harden the plants.

The plants are usually set on top of ridges, 3½ to 4 feet apart, with the plants about 12 inches apart in the row. When the vines have covered the ground, no further cultivation is necessary, but some additional hand weeding may be required.

Dig sweetpotatoes a short time before frost, on a bright, drying day when the soil is not too wet to work easily. On a small scale they may be dug with a spading fork, great care being taken not to bruise or injure the roots. Let the roots lie exposed for 2 or 3 hours to dry thoroughly; then put them in containers and place them in a warm room to cure. The proper curing temperature is 85° F. Curing for about 10 days is followed by storage at 50° to 55°.

Turnip and Rutabaga

Turnips and rutabagas, similar cool-season vegetables, are among the most commonly grown and widely adapted root crops in the United States. They are grown in the South chiefly in the fall, winter, and spring; in the North, largely in the spring and autumn. Rutabagas do best in the more northerly areas; turnips are better for gardens south of the latitude of Indianapolis, Ind., or northern Virginia.

Turnips reach a good size in from 60 to 80 days, but rutabagas need about a month longer. Being susceptible to heat and hardy to cold, these crops should be planted as late as possible for fall use, allowing time for maturity before hard frost. In the South, turnips are very popular in the winter and spring. In the North, however, July to August seeding, following early potatoes, peas, or spinach, is the common practice.

Land that has been in a heavily fertilized crop, such as early potatoes, usually gives a good crop without additional fertilizing. The soil need not be prepared deeply, but the surface should be fine and smooth. For spring culture, row planting similar to that described for beets is the best practice. The importance of planting turnips as early as possible for the spring crop is emphasized. When seeding in rows, cover the seeds lightly; when broadcasting, rake the seeds in lightly with a garden rake. A half ounce of seed will sow a 300-foot row or broadcast 300 square feet. Turnips may be thinned as they grow, and the tops used for greens.

Although there are both white-fleshed and yellow-fleshed varieties of turnips and rutabagas, most turnips are white-fleshed and most rutabagas are yellow-fleshed. Purple Top White Globe and Just Right are the most popular white-fleshed varieties; Golden Ball (Orange Jelly) is the most popular yellow-fleshed variety. American Purple Top is the commonly grown yellow-fleshed rutabaga; Sweet German (White Swede, Sweet Russian) is the most widely used white-fleshed variety. For turnip greens, the Seven Top variety is most suitable. This winter-hardy variety overwinters in a majority of locations in the United States.

Turnip-Rooted Parsley

The root is the edible portion of turnip-rooted parsley. The flesh is whitish and dry, with much the same flavor as celeriac.

Turnip-rooted parsley requires the same climate, soil, and culture as parsley. It can withstand much cold, but is difficult to start in dry, hot weather. This vegetable may remain in the ground until after hard frosts. It may be lifted and stored like other root crops.

Vine Vegetables

The vine crops, including cucumbers, muskmelons, pumpkins, squashes, watermelons, and citrons, are similar in their cultural requirements. In importance to the home gardener they do not compare with some other groups, especially the root crops and the greens, but there is a place in most gardens for at least bush squashes and a few hills of cucumbers. They all make rank growth and require much space. In large gardens, muskmelons and watermelons are often desirable.

Cucumber

Cucumbers are a warm-weather crop. They may be grown during the warmer months over a wide portion of the country, but are not adapted to winter growing in any but a few of the most southerly locations. Moreover, the extreme heat of midsummer in some places is too severe, and there cucumber culture is limited to spring and autumn.

The cucumber demands an exceedingly fertile, mellow soil high in decomposed organic matter from the compost pile. Also, an additional application of organic matter and commercial fertilizer is advisable under the rows or hills. Be sure the organic matter contains no remains of any vine crops; they might carry injurious diseases. Three or four wheelbarrow loads of well-rotted organic matter and 5 pounds of commercial fertilizer to a 50-foot drill or each 10 hills are enough. Mix the organic matter and fertilizer well with the top 8 to 10 inches of soil.

For an early crop, the seed may be started in berry boxes or pots, or on sods in a hotbed, and moved to the garden after danger of late frost is past. During the early growth and in cool periods, cucumbers may be covered with plant protectors made of panes of glass with a top of cheesecloth, parchment paper, or muslin. A few hills will supply the needs of a family.

When the seed is planted in drills, the rows should be 6 or 7 feet apart, with the plants thinned to 2 to 3 feet apart in the rows. In the hill method of planting, the hills should be at least 6 feet apart each way, with the plants thinned to 2 in each hill. It is always wise to plant 8 or 10 seeds in each hill, thinned to the desired stand. Cover the seeds to a depth of about ½ inch. If the soil is inclined to bake, cover them with loose earth, such as a mixture of soil and coarse sand, or other material that will not harden and keep the plants from coming through.

When cucumbers are grown primarily for pickling, plant one of the special small-size pickling varieties, such as Chicago Pickling or National Pickling; if they are grown for slicing, plant such varieties as White Spine or Straight Eight. It is usually desirable to plant a few hills of each type; both types can be used for either purpose.

Cucumbers require almost constant vigilance to prevent destructive attacks by cucumber beetles. These insects not only eat the foliage but also spread cucumber wilt and other serious diseases.

Success in growing cucumbers depends largely on the control of diseases and insect pests that attack the crop.

Removal of the fruits before any hard seeds form materially lengthens the life of the plants and increases the size of the crop.

Gourd

Gourds have the same general habit of growth as pumpkins and squashes and should have the same general cultural treatment, except that most species require some form of support or trellis to climb upon.

Gourds are used in making dippers, spoons, ladles, salt and sugar containers, and many other kinds of household utensils. They are also used for birdhouses and the manufacture of calabash pipes. But they are of interest chiefly because of their ornamental and decorative possibilities (Fig. 19). The thin-shelled, or hard-drying, gourds are the most durable and are the ones that most commonly serve as decorations. The thick-fleshed gourds are more in the nature of pumpkins and squashes, and are almost as perishable.

The thin-shelled gourds of the Lagenaria group are gathered and cured at the time the shells begin to harden, the fruits become lighter in weight, and the tendrils on the vines near the gourds begin to shrivel and dry. For best results, give the gourds plenty of time to cure. Some kinds require 6 months or a year to cure.

The thick-shelled gourds of the Cucurbita group are more difficult to cure than the thin-shelled ones. Their beauty is of short duration; they usually begin to fade after 3 or 4 months.

All types of gourds should be handled care-

Figure 19.—An assorted collection of ornamental gourds.

fully. Bruises discolor them and cause them to soften and decay.

Muskmelon

The climatic, soil, and cultural requirements of muskmelons are about the same as for cucumbers, except that they are less tolerant of high humidity and rainy weather. They develop most perfectly on light-textured soils. The plants are vigorous growers, and need a somewhat wider spacing than cucumbers.

Hearts of Gold, Hale's Best, and Rocky Ford, the last-named a type not a variety, are usually grown in the home garden. Where powdery mildew is prevalent, resistant varieties such as Gulf Stream, Dulce, and Perlita are better adapted. Osage and Pride of Wisconsin (Queen of Colorado) are desirable home-garden sorts, particularly in the Northern States. Sweet Air (Knight) is a popular sort in the Maryland-Virginia area.

The Casaba and Honey Dew are well adapted only to the West, where they are grown under irrigation.

Pumpkin

Pumpkins are sensitive to both cold and heat. In the North, they cannot be planted until settled weather; in the South they do not thrive during midsummer.

The gardener is seldom jusified in devoting any part of a limited garden area to pumpkins, because many other vegetables give greater returns from the same space. However, in gardens where there is plenty of room and where they can follow an early crop like potatoes, pumpkins can often be grown to advantage.

The pumpkin is one of the few vegetables that thrives under partial shade. Therefore it may be grown among sweet corn or other tall plants. Small Sugar and Connecticut Field are well-known orange-yellow-skinned varieties. The Kentucky Field has a grayish-orange rind with salmon flesh. All are good-quality, productive varieties.

Hills of pumpkins, containing one to two plants, should be at least 10 feet apart each way. Pumpkin plants among corn, potato, or other plants usually should be spaced 8 to 10 feet apart in every third or fourth row.

Gather and store pumpkins before they are injured by hard frosts. They keep best in a well-ventilated place where the temperature is a little above 50° F.

Squash

Squashes are among the most commonly grown garden plants. They do well in practically all parts of the United States where the soil is fertile and moisture sufficient. Although sensitive to frost, squashes are more hardy than melons and cucumbers. In the warmest parts of the South they may be grown in winter. The use of well-rotted composted material thoroughly mixed with the soil is recommended.

There are two classes of squash varieties, summer and winter. The summer class includes the Bush Scallop, known in some places as the Cymling, the Summer Crookneck, Straightneck, and Zucchini. It also includes the vegetable marrows, of which the best known sort is Italian Vegetable Marrow (Cocozelle). All the summer squashes and the marrows must be used while young and tender, when the rind can be easily penetrated by the thumbnail. The winter squashes include varieties such as Hubbard, Delicious, Table Queen (Acorn), and Boston Marrow. They have hard rinds and are well adapted for storage.

Summer varieties, like yellow Straightneck (fig. 20), should be gathered before the seeds ripen or the rinds harden, but the winter sorts will not keep unless well-matured. They should be taken in before hard frosts and stored in a dry, moderately warm place, such as on shelves in a basement with a furnace. Under favorable conditions such varieties as Hubbard may be kept until midwinter.

Watermelon

Only gardeners with a great deal of space can afford to grow watermelons. Moreover, they are rather particular in their soil requirements, a sand or sandy loam being best. Watermelon hills should be at least 8 feet apart. The plan of mixing a half wheelbarrow load of composted material with the soil in each hill is good, provided the compost is free from the

Figure 20.—A mulched plant of Yellow Straightneck summer squash.

remains of cucurbit plants that might carry diseases. A half pound of commercial fertilizer also should be thoroughly mixed with the soil in the hill. It is a good plan to place several seeds in a ring about 1 foot in diameter in each hill. Later the plants should be thinned to two to each hill.

New Hampshire Midget, Rhode Island Red, and Charleston Gray are suitable varieties for the home garden. New Hampshire Midget and Sugar Baby are small, extra early, widely grown, very productive varieties. The oval fruits are about 5 inches in diameter; they have crisp, red flesh and dark seeds. Rhode Island Red is an early variety. The fruits are medium in size, striped, and oval; they have a firm rind and bright pink-red flesh of choice quality. Charleston Gray is a large, long, high-quality, gray-green watermelon with excellent keeping and shipping qualities. It is resistant to anthracnose and fusarium wilt and requires a long growing season.

The preserving type of watermelon—citron—is not edible when raw. Its culture is the same as that for watermelon.

Legumes

Beans and peas are among our oldest and most important garden plants. The popularity of both is enhanced by their wide climatic and soil adaptation.

Beans

Green beans, both snap and lima, are more important than dry beans to the home gardener. Snap beans cannot be planted until the ground is thoroughly warm, but succession plantings may be made every 2 weeks from that time until 7 or 8 weeks before frost. In the lower South and Southwest, green beans may be grown during the fall, winter, and spring, but they are not well adapted to midsummer. In the extreme South, beans are grown throughout the winter.

Green beans are adapted to a wide range of soils as long as the soils are well drained, reasonably fertile, and of such physical nature that they do not interfere with germination and emergence of the plants. Soil that has received a general application of manure and fertilizer should need no additional fertiliza-

tion. When beans follow early crops that have been fertilized, the residue of this fertilizer is often sufficient for the beans.

On very heavy lands it is well to cover the planted row with sand, a mixture of sifted coal ashes and sand, peat, leafmold, or other material that will not bake. Bean seed should be covered not more than 1 inch in heavy soils and 1½ inches in sandy soils. When beans are planted in hills, they may be covered with plant protectors. These covers make it possible to plant somewhat earlier.

Tendercrop (fig. 21), Topcrop, Tenderette, Contender, Harvester, and Kinghorn Wax are good bush varieties of snap beans. Dwarf Horticultural is an outstanding green-shell bean. Brown-seeded or white-seeded Kentucky Wonders are the best pole varieties for snap pods.

Figure 21.—Tendercrop is a mosaic-resistant, heavy yielding snap bean with tender, round, green pods and a wide range of adaptability.

White Navy, or pea beans, white or red Kidney, and the horticultural types are excellent for dry-shell purposes.

Two types of lima beans, called butter beans in the South, are grown in home gardens. Most of the more northerly parts of the United States, including the northern New England States and the northern parts of other States along the Canadian border, are not adapted to the culture of lima beans. Lima beans need a growing season of about 4 months with relatively high temperature; they cannot be planted safely until somewhat later than snap beans. The small butter beans mature in a shorter period than the large-seeded lima beans. The use of plant protectors over the seeds is an aid in obtaining earliness.

Lima beans may be grown on almost any fertile, well-drained, mellow soil, but it is especially desirable that the soil be light-textured and not subject to baking, as the seedlings cannot force their way through a hard crust. Covering with some material that will not bake, as suggested for other beans, is a wise precaution when using heavy soils. Lima beans need a soil somewhat richer than is necessary for kidney beans, but the excessive use of fertilizer containing a high percentage of nitrogen should be avoided.

Both the small- and large-seeded lima beans are available in pole and bush varieties. In the South, the most commonly grown lima bean varieties are Jackson Wonder, Nemagreen, Henderson Bush, and Sieva pole; in the North, Thorogreen, Dixie Butterpea, and Thaxter are popular small-seeded bush varieties. Fordhook 242 (fig. 22) is the most popular midseason large, thick-seeded bush lima bean. King of the Garden and Challenger are the most popular large-seeded pole lima bean varieties.

Pole beans of the kidney and lima types require some form of support, as they normally make vines several feet long. A 5-foot fence makes the best support for pole beans. A more complicated support can be prepared from 8-foot metal fence posts, spaced about 4 feet apart and connected horizontally and diagonally with coarse stout twine to make a trellis. Bean plants usually require some assistance to get started on these supports. Never cultivate

Figure 22.—Fordhook 242 bush lima beans are vigorous, productive, and heat-resistant.

or handle bean plants when they are wet; to do so is likely to spread disease.

English Peas

English peas are a cool-weather crop and should be planted early. In the lower South they are grown at all seasons except summer; farther north, in spring and autumn. In the Northern States and at high altitudes, they may be grown from spring until autumn, although in many places summer heat is too severe and the season is practically limited to spring. A few succession plantings may be made at 10-day intervals. The later plantings rarely yield as well as the earlier ones. Planting may be resumed as the cool weather of autumn approaches, but the yield is seldom as satisfactory as that from the spring planting.

Alaska and other smooth-seeded varieties are frequently used for planting in the early spring because of the supposition that they can germinate well in cold, wet soil. Thomas Laxton, Greater Progress, Little Marvel, Freezonia, and Giant Stride are recommended as suitable early varieties with wrinkled seeds. Wando has considerable heat resistance. Alderman and Lincoln are approximately 2 weeks later than Greater Progress, but under favorable conditions yield heavily. Alderman is a desirable variety for growing on brush or a trellis. Peas grown on supports are less liable to destruction by birds.

Sugar Peas

Sugar peas (edible podded peas) possess the tenderness and fleshy podded qualities of snap beans and the flavor and sweetness of fresh English peas. When young, the pods are cooked like snap beans; the peas are not shelled. At this stage, pods are stringless, brittle, succulent, and free of fiber or parchment. However, if the pods develop too fast, they are not good to use like snap beans, but the seeds may be eaten as shelled peas and are of the best flavor before they have reached full size. Dwarf Gray Sugar is the earliest and dwarfest sugar pea. It is ideal for home gardens, especially where space is limited and seasons are short. A larger and later variety, Mammoth Melting Sugar, is resistant to fusarium wilt and requires support to climb upon.

Blackeye Peas

Blackeye peas, also known as cowpeas or Southern table peas, are highly nutritious, tasty, and easily grown. Do not plant until danger of frost has passed because they are very susceptible to cold. Leading varieties are Dixilee, Brown Crowder, Lady, Conch, White Acre, Louisiana Purchase, Texas Purple Hull 49, Knuckle Purple Hull, and Monarch Blackeye. Dixilee is a later variety of southern pea. Quality is excellent and it yields considerably more than such old standbys as blackeyes and crowders. It is also quite resistant, or at least tolerant, to nematodes. This fact alone makes it a desirable variety wherever this pest is present. Monarch Blackeye is a fairly new variety of the blackeye type and much better adapted to southern conditions.

Heavy applications of nitrogen fertilizer should not be used for southern peas. Fertilize moderately with a low-nitrogen analysis such as 4–12–12.

For the effort necessary to grow them, few if any other vegetables will pay higher dividends than Southern table peas.

Soybeans

The soil and cultural requirements and methods of growing soybeans are essentially the same as for bush forms of common beans. Soybeans, however, are slower growing than most garden beans, requiring 3 to 5 months for maturity, and warmer weather. They also are taller growing, the larger, later varieties requiring a greater distance between rows than dwarf snap beans. Small, early varieties may be planted in rows as close as 2 feet, but the larger, later ones require 3 feet between rows. The planting dates given in tables 4 and 5 are for midseason varieties (about 120 days), neither the earliest nor the latest kinds. Differences in time of development among varieties are so great that the gardener must choose the proper variety and know its time of maturity in making plans for planting in any particular locality. Kanrich and Giant Green are the most widely grown varieties.

In cooler sections the rate of development will be slower. Only the early varieties should be grown in the more northerly States, and the medium or late varieties in the South. Plantings should be made principally when tomatoes and other long-season, warm-weather crops are put in the garden.

For use as a green vegetable, soybean pods should be harvested when the seeds are fully grown but before the pods turn yellow. Most varieties produce beans in usable condition over a period of a week to 10 days. The green beans are difficult to remove from the pods unless the pods are boiled or steamed 4 to 5 minutes, after which they are easily shelled.

The yields per unit area of land are about the same as are usually obtained with peas and are thus less than can be obtained with many other vegetables. On this account, they appear of major interest only to gardeners having medium to large gardens.

Cabbage Group

The cabbage, or cole, group of vegetables is noteworthy because of its adaptation to culture in most parts of the country having fertile soil and sufficient moisture and because of its hardiness to cold.

Broccoli

Heading broccoli is difficult to grow, therefore, only sprouting broccoli is discussed here. Sprouting broccoli forms a loose flower head (on a tall, green, fleshy, branching stalk) instead of a compact head or curd found on cauliflower or heading broccoli. It is one of the

39

newer vegetables in American gardens, but has been grown by Europeans for hundreds of years.

Sprouting broccoli is adapted to winter culture in areas suitable for winter cabbage. It is also tolerant of heat. Spring-set plants in the latitude of Washington, D.C., have yielded good crops of sprouts until midsummer and later under conditions that caused cauliflower to fail. In the latitude of Norfolk, Va., the plant has yielded good crops of sprouts from December until spring.

Sprouting broccoli is grown in the same way as cabbage. Plants grown indoors in the early spring and set in the open about April 1 begin to yield sprouts about 10 weeks later. The fall crop may be handled in the same way as late cabbage, except that the seed is sown later. The sprouts carrying flower buds are cut about 6 inches long, and other sprouts arise in the axils of the leaves, so that a continuous harvest may be obtained (fig. 23). Green Comet, Calabrese, and Waltham 29 are among the best known varieties.

Brussels Sprouts

Brussels sprouts are somewhat more hardy than cabbage and will live outdoors over winter

Figure 23.—Sprouting broccoli with center head and side shoots.

in all the milder sections of the country. They may be grown as a winter crop in the South and as early and late as cabbage in the North. The sprouts, or small heads, are formed in the axils (the angle between the leaf stem and the main stalk) of the leaves. As the heads begin to crowd, break the lower leaves from the stem of the plant to give them more room. Always leave the top leaves; the plant needs them to supply nourishment. For winter use in cold areas, take up the plants that are well laden with heads and set them close together in a pit, a cold-frame, or a cellar, with some soil tamped around the roots. Keep the stored plants as cool as possible without freezing. Jade Cross, a true F_1 hybrid, has a wide range of adaptability.

Cabbage

Cabbage ranks as one of the most important home-garden crops. In the lower South, it can be grown in all seasons except summer, and in latitudes as far north as Washington, D.C., it is frequently set in the autumn, as its extreme hardiness enables it to live over winter at relatively low temperatures and thus become one of the first spring garden crops. Farther north, it can be grown as an early summer crop and as a late fall crop for storage. Cabbage can be grown throughout practically the entire United States.

Cabbage is adapted to widely different soils as long as they are fertile, of good texture, and moist. It is a heavy feeder; no vegetable responds better to favorable growing conditions. Quality in cabbage is closely associated with quick growth. Both compost and commercial fertilizer should be liberally used. In addition to the applications made at planting time, a side dressing or two of nitrate of soda, sulfate of ammonia, or other quickly available nitrogenous fertilizer is advisable. These may be applied sparingly to the soil around the plants at intervals of 3 weeks, not more than 1 pound being used to each 200 square feet of space, or, in terms of single plants, 1/3 ounce to each plant. For late cabbage the supplemental feeding with nitrates may be omitted. Good seed is especially important. Only a few seed is needed for starting enough plants for the home garden, as 2 or 3 dozen heads of early cabbage are as many as the average family can use. Early

Jersey Wakefield and Golden Acre are standard early sorts. Copenhagen Market and Globe are excellent midseason kinds. Flat Dutch and Danish Ballhead are largely used for late planting.

Where cabbage yellows is a serious disease, resistant varieties should be used. The following are a few of the wilt-resistant varieties adapted to different seasons: Wisconsin Hollander, for late storage; Wisconsin All Seasons, a kraut cabbage, somewhat earlier; Marion Market and Globe, round-head cabbages, for midseason; and Stonehead for an early, small, round-head variety.

Cabbage plants for spring setting in the North may be grown in hotbeds or greenhouses from seeding made a month to 6 weeks before planting time, or may be purchased from southern growers who produce them outdoors in winter. The winter-grown, hardened plants, sometimes referred to as frostproof, are hardier than hotbed plants and may be set outdoors in most parts of the North as soon as the ground can be worked in the spring. Northern gardeners can have cabbage from their gardens much earlier by using healthy southern-grown plants or well-hardened, well-grown hotbed or greenhouse plants. Late cabbage, prized by northern gardeners for fall use and for storage, is grown from plants produced in open seedbeds from sowings made about a month ahead of planting. Late cabbage may well follow early potatoes, peas, beets, spinach, or other early crop. Many gardeners set cabbage plants between potato rows before the potatoes are ready to dig, thereby gaining time. In protected places, or when plant protectors are used, it is possible always to advance dates somewhat, especially if the plants are well hardened.

Chinese Cabbage

Chinese cabbage, (fig. 24) is more closely related to mustard than to cabbage. It is variously called Crispy Choy, Chihili, Michili, and Wong Bok. Also, it is popularly known as celery cabbage, although it is unrelated to celery. The nonheading types deserve greater attention.

Chinese cabbage seems to do best as an autumn crop in the northern tier of States. When fullgrown, it is an attractive vegetable. It is not especially successful as a spring crop,

Figure 24.—Chinese cabbage is a desirable autumn crop in the Northern States.

and gardeners are advised not to try to grow it at any season other than fall in the North or in winter in the South.

The plant demands a very rich, well-drained but moist soil. The seeds may be sown and the plants transplanted to the garden, or the seed may be drilled in the garden rows and the plants thinned to the desired stand.

Cauliflower

Cauliflower (fig. 25) is a hardy vegetable but it will not withstand as much frost as cabbage. Too much warm weather keeps cauliflower from heading. In the South, its culture is limited to fall, winter, and spring; in the North, to spring and fall. However, in some areas of high altitude and when conditions are otherwise favorable, cauliflower culture is continuous throughout the summer.

Cauliflower is grown on all types of land from sands to clay and peats. Although the physical character is unimportant, the land must be fertile and well drained. Manure and commercial fertilizer are essential.

The time required for growing cauliflower plants is the same as for cabbage. In the North, the main cause of failure with cauliflower in the spring is delay in sowing the seed and setting the plants. The fall crop must be planted at such a time that it will come to the heading stage in cool weather. Snowball and Purple Head are standard varieties of cauliflower. Snow King is an extremely early variety with

41

Figure 25.—A good head of cauliflower on a plant mulched with hay.

fair sized, compact heads of good quality; it has very short stems. Always take care to obtain a good strain of seed; poor cauliflower seed is most objectionable. The Purple Head variety, well adapted for the home garden, turns green when cooked.

A necessary precaution in cauliflower culture with all varieties, except Purple Head, is to tie the leaves together when the heads, or buttons, begin to form. This keeps the heads white. Cauliflower does not keep long after the heads form; 1 or 2 dozen heads are enough for the average garden in one season.

Kohlrabi

Kohlrabi is grown for its swollen stem. In the North, the early crop may be started like cabbage and transplanted to the garden, but usually it is sown in place. In the South, kohlrabi may be grown almost any time except midsummer. The seeds may be started indoors and the plants transplanted in the garden; or the seeds may be drilled in the garden rows and the plants thinned to the desired stand. Kohlrabi has about the same soil and cultural requirements as cabbage, principally a fertile soil and enough moisture. It should be harvested while young and tender. Standard varieties are Purple Vienna and White Vienna.

Onion Group

Practically all members of the onion group are adapted to a wide variety of soils. Some of them can be grown at one time of the year or another in any part of the country that has fertile soil and ample moisture. They require but little garden space to produce enough for a family's needs.

Chives

Chives are small onionlike plants (fig. 26) that will grow in any place where onions do well. They are frequently planted as a border, but are equally well adapted to culture in rows. Being a perennial, chives should be planted where they can be left for more than one season.

Chives may be started from either seed or clumps of bulbs. Once established, some of the bulbs can be lifted and moved to a new spot. When left in the same place for several years the plants become too thick; occasionally dividing and resetting is desirable.

Garlic

Garlic is more exacting in its cultural requirements than are onions, but it may be grown with a fair degree of success in almost

Figure 26.—A pot of chives grown in a kitchen window.

42

any home garden where good results are obtained with onions.

Garlic is propagated by planting the small cloves, or bulbs, which make up the large bulbs. Each large bulb contains about 10 small ones. Carefully separate the small bulbs and plant them singly.

The culture of garlic is practically the same as that of onions. When mature the bulbs are pulled, dried, and braided into strings or tied in bunches, which are hung in a cool, well-ventilated place.

In the South, where the crop matures early, care must be taken to keep the garlic in a cool, dry place; otherwise it spoils. In the North, where the crop matures later in the season, storage is not so difficult, but care must be taken to prevent freezing.

Leek

The leek resembles the onion in its adaptability and cultural requirements. Instead of forming a bulb it produces a thick, fleshy cylinder like a large green onion (fig. 27). Leeks are started from seeds, like onions. Usually the seeds are sown in a shallow trench, so that the plants can be more easily hilled up as growth proceeds. Leeks are ready for use any time after they reach the right size. Under favorable conditions they grow to 1½ inches or

Figure 27.—Leeks are used for almost any purpose that onions are used for.

more in diameter, with white parts 6 to 8 inches long. They may be lifted in the autumn and stored like celery in a coldframe or a cellar.

Onion

Onions thrive under a wide variety of climatic and soil conditions, but do best with an abundance of moisture and a temperate climate, without extremes of heat or cold through the growing season. In the South, the onion thrives in the fall, winter, and spring. Farther north, winter temperatures may be too severe for certain types. In the North, onions are primarily a spring, summer, and fall crop.

Any type of soil will grow onions, but it must be fertile, moist, and in the highest state of tilth. Both compost and commercial fertilizer, especially one high in phosphorus and potash, should be applied to the onion plot. A pound of compost to each square foot of ground and 4 or 5 pounds of fertilizer to each 100 square feet are about right. The soil should be very fine and free from clods and foreign matter.

Onions may be started in the home garden by the use of sets, seedlings, or seed. Sets, or small dry onions grown the previous year—preferably not more than ¾ inch in diameter—are usually employed by home gardeners. Small green plants grown in an outdoor seedbed in the South or in a hotbed or a greenhouse are also in general use. The home-garden culture of onions from seed is satisfactory in the North where the summers are comparatively cool.

Sets and seedlings cost about the same; seeds cost much less. In certainty of results the seedlings are best; practically none form seedstalks. Seed-sown onions are uncertain unless conditions are extremely favorable.

Several distinct types of onions may be grown. The Potato (Multiplier) and Top (Tree) onions are planted in the fall or early spring for use green. Yellow Bermuda, Granex, and White Granex are large, very mild, flat onions for spring harvest in the South; they have short storage life. Sweet Spanish and the hybrids Golden Beauty, Fiesta, Bronze, Perfection, El Capitan are large, mild, globular onions suited for growing in the middle latitudes of the country; they store moderately well. Southport White Globe, Southport Yellow Globe, Ebenezer, Early Yellow Globe, Yellow

Globe Danvers, and the hybrid Abundance are all firm-fleshed, long-storage onions for growing as a "main crop" in the Northeast and Midwest. Early Harvest is an early F_1 hybrid adapted to all northern regions of the United States. Varieties that produce bulbs may also be used green.

Shallot

The shallot is a small onion of the Multiplier type. Its bulbs have a more delicate flavor than most onions. Its growth requirements are about the same as those of most other onions. Shallots seldom form seed and are propagated by means of the small cloves or divisions, into which the plant splits during growth. The plant is hardy and may be left in the ground from year to year, but best results are had by lifting the clusters of bulbs at the end of the growing season and replanting the smaller ones at the desired time.

Fleshy-Fruited Vegetables

The fleshy-fruited, warm-season vegetables, of which the tomato is the most important, are closely related and have about the same cultural requirements. All must have warm weather and fertile, well-drained soil for good results.

Eggplant

Eggplant is extremely sensitive to the conditions under which it is grown. A warm-weather plant, it demands a growing season of from 100 to 140 days with high average day and night temperatures. The soil, also, must be well warmed up before eggplant can safely be set outdoors.

In the South, eggplants are grown in spring and autumn; in the North, only in summer. The more northerly areas, where a short growing season and low summer temperatures prevail, are generally unsuitable for eggplants. In very fertile garden soil, which is best for eggplant, a few plants will yield a large number of fruits.

Sow eggplant seeds in a hotbed or greenhouse, or, in warm areas, outdoors about 8 weeks before the plants are to be transplanted. It is important that the plants be kept growing without check from low or drying temperatures

or other causes. They may be transplanted like tomatoes. Good plants have stems that are not hard or woody; one with a woody stem rarely develops satisfactorily. Black Beauty (fig. 28), Early Beauty Hybrid, and Jersey King Hybrid are good varieties.

Pepper

Peppers are more exacting than tomatoes in their requirements, but may be grown over a wide range in the United States. Being hot-weather plants, peppers cannot be planted in the North until the soil has warmed up and all danger of frost is over. In the South, planting dates vary with the location, fall planting being practiced in some locations. Start pepper plants 6 to 8 weeks before needed. The seeds and plants require a somewhat higher temperature than those of the tomato. Otherwise they are handled in exactly the same way.

Hot peppers are represented by such varieties as Red Chili and Long Red Cayenne; the mild-flavored by Penn Wonder, Ruby King, World-beater, California Wonder (fig. 29), and Yale Wonder, which mature in the order given.

Tomato

Tomatoes grow under a wide variety of conditions and require only a relatively small space for a large production. Of tropical American origin, the tomato does not thrive in very cool weather. It will, however, grow in winter in home gardens in the extreme South. Over most of the upper South and the North, it is suited to spring, summer, and autumn culture. In the

Figure 28.—The eggplant is a popular vegetable that requires little space.

44

Figur 29.—California Wonder variety of pepper.

more northern areas, the growing season is likely to be too short for heavy yields, and it is often desirable to increase earliness and the length of the growing season by starting the plants indoors. By adopting a few precautions, the home gardener can grow tomatoes practically everywhere, given fertile soil with sufficient moisture.

A liberal application of compost and commercial fertilizer in preparing the soil should be sufficient for tomatoes under most conditions. Heavy applications of fertilizer should be broadcast, not applied in the row; but small quantities may be mixed with the soil in the row in preparing for planting.

Start early tomato plants from 5 to 7 weeks before they are to be transplanted to the garden. Enough plants for the home garden may be started in a window box and transplanted to small pots, paper drinking cups with the bottoms removed, plant bands (round or square), or other soil containers. In boxes, the seedlings are spaced 2 to 3 inches apart. Tomato seeds germinate best at about 70° F., or ordinary house temperature. Growing tomato seedlings, after the first transplanting, at moderate temperatures, with plenty of ventilation, as in a coldframe, gives stocky, hardy growth. If desired, the plants may be transplanted again to larger containers, such as 4-inch clay pots or quart cans with holes in the bottom.

Tomato plants for all but the early spring crop are usually grown in outdoor seedbeds. Thin seeding and careful weed control will give strong, stocky plants for transplanting. A list of tomato varieties for home garden use in areas other than the Southwest is given in table 6.

In the Southwest, Pearson, Early Pack No. 7, VF 36, California 145, VF 13L, and Ace are grown.

Tomatoes are sensitive to cold. Never plant them until danger of frost is past. By using plant protectors during cool periods the home gardener can set tomato plants somewhat earlier than would otherwise be possible. Hot, dry weather, like mid-summer weather in the South is also unfavorable for planting tomatoes. Planting distances depend on the variety and on whether the plants are to be pruned and staked or not. If pruned to one stem, trained, and tied to stakes or a trellis, they may be set 18 inches apart in 3-foot rows (fig. 30); if not, they may be planted 3 feet apart in rows 4 to 5

Figure 30.—Tomato plants staked with a wire cylinder to hold them off the ground so the fruit does not rot. The grass mulch around the plants controls weeds and conserves moisture.

45

TABLE 6.—*Tomato varieties for areas other than the Southwest*

Variety	Area
Ace	West
Atkinson	South
C17	East, Midwest
Fireball VF	East, North
Floradel	South
R1350	East, Midwest
Homestead–24	South
Manalucie	South
Marion	South
Morton Hybrid	North, East
Moscow VR	West
Small Fry	All areas
Spring Giant	East, Midwest
Supermarket	South
Supersonic	East, Midwest
Tropi-Gro	South
VFW-8	West

feet apart. Pruning and staking have many advantages for the home gardener. Cultivation is easier, and the fruits are always clean and easy to find. Staked and pruned tomatoes are, however, more subject to losses from blossom-end rot than those allowed to grow naturally.

Miscellaneous Vegetables

Florence Fennel

Florence fennel is related to celery and celeriac. Its enlarged, flattened leafstalk is the portion used. For a summer crop, sow the seeds in the rows in spring; for an autumn and winter crop in the South, sow them toward the end of the summer. Thin the plants to stand about 6 inches apart. When the leafstalks have grown to about 2 inches in diameter the plants may be slightly mounded up and partially blanched. They should be harvested and used before they become tough and stringy.

Okra

Okra, or gumbo, has about the same degree of hardiness as cucumbers and tomatoes and may be grown under the same conditions. It thrives on any fertile, well-drained soil. An abundance of quickly available plant food will stimulate growth and insure a good yield of tender, high-quality pods.

As okra is a warm-weather vegetable, the seeds should not be sown until the soil is warm. The rows should be from 3 to 3½ feet apart, depending on whether the variety is dwarf or large growing. Sow the seeds every few inches and thin the plants to stand 18 inches to 2 feet apart in the rows. Clemson Spineless, Emerald, and Dwarf Green are good varieties. The pods should be picked young and tender, and none allowed to ripen. Old pods are unfit for use and soon exhaust the plant.

Physalis

Physalis known also as groundcherry and husk tomato, is closely related to the tomato and can be grown wherever tomatoes do well. The kind ordinarily grown in gardens produces a yellow fruit about the size of a cherry. The seeds may be started indoors or sown in rows in the garden.

Sweet Corn

Sweet corn requires plenty of space and is adapted only to the larger gardens. Although a warm-weather plant, it may be grown in practically all parts of the United States. It needs a fertile, well-drained, moist soil. With these requirements met, the type of the soil does not seem to be especially important, but a clay loam is almost ideal for sweet corn.

In the South, sweet corn is planted from early spring until autumn, but the corn earworm, drought, and heat make it difficult to obtain worthwhile results in midsummer. The ears pass the edible stage very quickly, and succession plantings are necessary to insure a constant supply. In the North, sweet corn cannot be safely planted until the ground has thoroughly warmed up. Here, too, succession plantings need to be made to insure a steady supply. Sweet corn is frequently planted to good advantage after early potatoes, peas, beets, lettuce, or other early, short-season crops. Sometimes, to gain time, it may be planted before the early crop is removed.

Sweet corn may be grown in either hills or drills, in rows at least 3 feet apart. It is well to plant the seed rather thickly and thin to single stalks 14 to 16 inches apart or three plants to each 3-foot hill. Experiments have shown that in the eastern part of the country there is no advantage in removing suckers from sweet corn. Cultivation sufficient to control weeds is all that is needed.

Hybrid sweet corn varieties, both white and

yellow, are usually more productive than the open-pollinated sorts. As a rule, they need a more fertile soil and heavier feeding. They should be fertilized with 5–10–5 fertilizer about every 3 weeks until they start to silk. Many are resistant to disease, particularly bacterial wilt. Never save seed from a hybrid crop for planting. Such seed does not come true to the form of the plants from which it was harvested.

Good yellow-grained hybrids, in the order of the time required to reach edible maturity, are Span-cross, Marcross, Golden Beauty, Golden Cross Bantam, and Ioana. White-grained hybrids are Evergreen and Country Gentleman.

Well-known open-pollinated yellow sorts are Golden Bantam and Golden Midget. Open-pollinated white sorts, in the order of maturity, are Early Evergreen, Country Gentleman, and Stowell Evergreen.

MINIGARDENS

You'd like to be a gardener, but you live in a room, an apartment, or a townhouse—and you think you have no place for a garden. But if you have a windowsill, a balcony, or a doorstep you have enough room for a minigarden.

Growing vegetables in a minigarden can be fun for youngsters as well as for the not-so-young. You don't need to be familiar with growing plants—not if you have the patience to follow a few instructions.

The basic materials you will need for minigardening are some containers, some synthetic soil, and some seeds.

A half-bushel basket offers a good, light container for growing vegetables.

Containers

To start a minigarden of vegetables, you will need a container large enough to hold the plant when it's fully grown. You can use plastic or clay pots, an old pail, a plastic bucket, a bushel basket, a wire basket, or a wooden box. Most any container is satisfactory—from tiny pots for your kitchen windowsill to large wooden boxes for your patio.

The size and number of the containers can vary with the space you have and the number of plants you want to grow. Six-inch pots are satisfactory for chives. Radishes, onion, and a variety of miniature tomato (Tiny Tim) will do well in 10-inch pots. For the average patio, 5-gallon plastic trash cans are suitable. They are easy to handle and provide enough space for the larger vegetable plants. Half-bushel or bushel baskets also work well if you have room for them.

Readymade containers of plastic, metal and wood are so widely available that it is not necessary to build your own containers. Many are designed especially for growing plants. Others can easily be modified for growing plants, particularly pails, tubs, baskets, and trash containers. Plastic laundry baskets, for example, are attractive and can be modified by lining them with plastic sheeting.

If you use solid plastic containers, allow for drainage. Drill four or more ¼-inch holes, spaced evenly along the sides, near the bottom. Don't drill the holes in the bottom itself. Then, to further help drainage, put about one-half inch of coarse gravel in the bottom of each container.

Wood containers, such as a bushel basket, will last 3 to 5 years if painted both inside and outside with a safe wood preservative.

peat moss, add 1¼ cups of ground limestone (preferably dolomitic), one-half cup of 20% superphosphate, and one cup of 5-10-5 fertilizer. This material should be mixed thoroughly. If the material is very dry, add a little water to it to reduce the dust during mixing.

Seeds

Your success in minigardening will depend partly on the quality of seed you plant. Vege-

Tomatoes probably offer the largest edible return for your time and effort if you have a sunny spot.

Synthetic Soil

You can buy a soil substitute, or synthetic soil, prepared from a mixture of horticultural vermiculite, peat moss, and fertilizer. This mixture, sold by seed dealers and garden supply centers, comes ready to use. For minigardening it has several advantages over soil. It is free of plant disease organisms and weed seeds, it holds moisture and plant nutrients well, and it is very lightweight and portable.

You can prepare your own soil substitute from horticultural grade vermiculite, peat moss, limestone, superphosphate, and 5-10-5 fertilizer. To one bushel each of vermiculite and shredded

table seed envelopes are stamped with the year in which they should be planted. So check the seed to see that it is not old. Old seed often germinates poorly and does not grow vigorously. Don't use last year's seed.

Seeds of many varieties of each plant are available. Miniature vegetable varieties are best for minigardens. When possible, select disease- and insect-resistant varieties.

Light

Vegetable plants grow better in full sunlight than in the shade. Some vegetables need more sun than others. Leafy vegetables (lettuce, cab-

49

Lettuce is a good minigarden crop. It is a fast-growing, cool-weather crop and can be grown in a small container without much sunlight.

Plastic bags make excellent containers for starting plants.

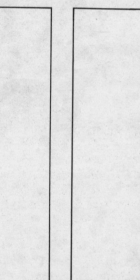

An old metal pail provides space for a pepper plant.

bage, mustard greens) can stand more shade than root vegetables (beets, radishes, turnips). Root vegetables can stand more shade than vegetable fruit plants (cucumbers, peppers, tomatoes), which do very poorly in the shade. Plant your vegetable fruit plants where they will get the most sun, and your leafy vegetables and root vegetables in the shadier areas.

Planting Dates

Planting or transplanting vegetables at the proper time helps insure success. The best planting date in one area may be days or weeks from the best date in another. This is because temperatures can differ greatly from one place to another—even a few miles apart. City temperatures, for example, are usually 5 to 10 degrees higher than those in the suburbs.

To follow the planting instructions given at the end of this chapter, you need to know—for your locality—the frost-free date in the spring and the average date of the first killing frost in the fall. Consult the tables in the chapter on vegetable growing for this information.

Starting Plants Indoors

You can give some plants a jump on the growing season by starting them indoors on windowsills that have plenty of sunlight. Then after the weather gets warmer, you can transplant them into larger containers and move them outdoors.

Start your plants in small aluminum baking pans, plastic trays, pots, or milk cartons.

comes up, pull out the less vigorous ones.

Transplant seedlings to larger containers when the first two leaves are fully developed. Water them thoroughly before transplanting. Be careful not to disturb the roots.

Hardening

Plants should be gradually "hardened," or toughened, for 2 weeks before being moved outdoors. This is done by withholding water and lowering the temperature. Hardening slows down the plant's rate of growth to prepare them to withstand such conditions as chilling, drying winds. or high temperature.

Lettuce, cabbage, and many other plants can be toughened to withstand frost; others, such as

Peat pellets are one of the best mediums for starting plants. Compressed pellet (left) is shown before water has been added. Moistened pellet (center) is shown with seedling in place. Plant growing from peat pellet (right) is ready to transplant to a larger container in which the plant will grow to harvest.

Use readymade peat pellets, or peat pots; both are available from garden supply centers. Peat pellets contain synthetic soil that swells up several times its original size when water is added.

Clean your containers with hot soapy water, rinse them well, and fill them with the peat pots or the peat pellets. If you use the pellets, add water and wait until they expand.

Make a planting hole with your finger or some tool to correct depth for the kind of seed you are planting. Put in two or three seeds. Cover the seeds with peat moss and moisten with water. Then enclose the container in a plastic bag until the seedlings emerge. If more than one seedling

tomatoes and peppers, cannot be hardened.

Diseases and Insects

Vegetables grown in minigardens are as susceptible to attack by diseases and insects as those grown in a garden plot. There are many commercially sold preparations that can be used to combat these pests. Your local garden supply center will carry those varieties that are suitable for the diseases and insects most commonly found in your area.

Fertilizer

Apply one level teaspoon of 5-10-5 fertilizer

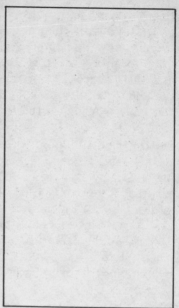

These lettuce seedlings are big enough to be transplanted into larger containers.

per square foot of soil about 3 weeks after the plants have reached the two-leaf stage and again every 3 weeks. Mix the fertilizer into the top one-half inch of the soil and water thoroughly. This will keep your plants growing rapidly and producing well.

Watering

Vegetables need a water supply equal to about one inch of rain every week during the growing season. Since you are gardening in containers, instead of a garden plot, you can control moisture easily. Water each time the soil becomes dry down to a depth of one-eighth inch. Overwatering will slowly kill your plants. During hot, dry weather you may need to water three times a week.

If you use a sprinkler can, do not water so late in the evening that the leaves of the plants stay wet at night. Wet leaves encourage plant diseases.

It is important for you to fill the bottom of your plant containers with gravel or similar material. This allows for good drainage. If your soil becomes waterlogged, the plants will die from lack of oxygen.

Cultivating

Weeds rob plants of water, nutrients, space and light. If weeds come up in your minigarden,

pull them by hand or use a small hand weeder to loosen the soil and remove the weeds while they are still small. Be careful not to injure the roots of your vegetable plants.

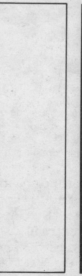

Radishes are the quickest and easiest crop to grow in a small space.

52

Guide to cultural requirements of vegetables

Plant	Light	When to plant	Days from seed to harvest	Space between plants (inches)	Planting depth (inches)	When to harvest
BEETS	Tolerate partial shade.	2 to 4 weeks before frost-free date.	50 to 60	2 to 3	½	When 1 to 2 inches in diameter.
CABBAGE	Tolerates partial shade.	Set out plants 4 to 6 weeks before frost-free date.	65 to 120, depending on variety.	12 to 18	½ (for seed); bury roots of plants.	When head is hard and rounded.

Comment: Thin plants when 6 to 8 inches high; use thinnings for greens.

Plant	Light	When to plant	Days from seed to harvest	Space between plants (inches)	Planting depth (inches)	When to harvest
CARROTS	Tolerate partial shade.	2 to 4 weeks before frost-free date.	65 to 80	2 to 3	½	For small carrots, when ½ to 1 inch in diameter.

Comment: Can also be set out for a fall crop.

Comment: To get several harvests, make plantings at 3-week intervals until 3 months before fall freezing date.

Plant	Light	When to plant	Days from seed to harvest	Space between plants (inches)	Planting depth (inches)	When to harvest
CHIVES	Grow in partial shade, as in kitchen window.	Set out plants 4 to 6 weeks before frost-free date (can also be started from seed).	60 to 70	2 to 3 (in clusters).	½	Clip as needed for salads, toppings.

Comment: Bulbs should be divided occasionally, so that they do not get too thick.

Plant	Light	When to plant	Days from seed to harvest	Space between plants (inches)	Planting depth (inches)	When to harvest
CUCUMBERS	Require full sunlight.	Set out plants 1 week after frost-free date.	70 to 80	18	½ (for seed); bury roots of plants.	For best yield, pick before hard seeds form.

Comment: Need hot weather. Use container of at least 5-gallon size. Start seeds in pots or berry boxes about 3 weeks before time to set out. During early growth, cover with a paper or plastic tent during cool nights.

Plant	Light	When to plant	Days from seed to harvest	Space between plants (inches)	Planting depth (inches)	When to harvest
EGGPLANT	Needs full sunlight.	Set out plants on frost-free date; they require warm soil.	100 to 140	One plant to a 3-gallon container.	½ (for seed); bury roots of plants.	When fruits are mature.

Comment: Hard to grow in northern part of U.S. because of high heat requirement and long growing season. Cover the plants during cool periods. You might want to try the new dwarf varieties. Start seeds indoors 8 to 9 weeks before transplanting time.

Plant	Light	When to plant	Days from seed to harvest	Space between plants (inches)	Planting depth (inches)	When to harvest
KALE	Tolerates partial shade.	6 to 8 weeks before first fall freeze.	55 to 70	6	½	When tall enough for greens; cut whole plants or take larger leaves.

Comment: Very winter hardy. Plant also in early fall for winter crops.

Crop	Light	Planting time	Days to maturity	Spacing (inches)	Depth (inches)	Harvest
LEEK	Tolerates partial shade.	4 to 6 weeks before frost-free date.	130	2 to 3	½	When 1 inch in diameter and white part is 5 to 6 inches long.

Comment: Leek is a decorative and winter-hardy plant.

Crop	Light	Planting time	Days to maturity	Spacing (inches)	Depth (inches)	Harvest
LEAF LETTUCE	Tolerates partial shade.	4 to 6 weeks before frost-free date and 6 to 8 weeks before first fall freeze.	30 to 35	4 to 6	¼	Cut leaves when large enough to use.

Comment: Lettuce is a cool-weather crop. It can be started inside early and set out even before frosts end. Plants will tolerate temperatures as low as 28° F. You can make several later plantings for summer lettuce unless hot weather hinders growth.

Crop	Light	Planting time	Days to maturity	Spacing (inches)	Depth (inches)	Harvest
MUSTARD GREENS	Tolerate partial shade.	2 to 4 weeks before frost-free date until 6 to 8 weeks before first fall freeze.	35 to 40	4 to 5	¼	When large enough to make greens.

Crop	Light	Planting time	Days to maturity	Spacing (inches)	Depth (inches)	Harvest
ONIONS	Green onions grow in partial shade; mature bulbs need full sun.	Plant bulb sets 4 to 6 weeks before frost-free date.	100 to 120 (less time for green onions).	2 to 3	1 to 1½	When large enough for green onions (8 to 10 inches tall); after they dry out they are usable as cooking onions.

Comment: Can be grown throughout the summer. You can make plantings at 10-day intervals for successive crops.

Comment: Onions like lots of moisture.

Crop	Light	Planting time	Days to maturity	Spacing (inches)	Depth (inches)	Harvest
PARSLEY	Does well in partial shade; will grow on kitchen windowsills.	Set out plants 4 to 6 weeks before frost-free date.	85	6 to 8	¼	Clip for garnish.

Comment: Sensitive to heat. Parsley seeds germinate slowly; soak them in water overnight before planting to keep soil moist. Start indoors if possible.

Crop	Light	Planting time	Days to maturity	Spacing (inches)	Depth (inches)	Harvest
PEPPERS	Require full sunlight.	Set out plants 1 week after frost-free date.	110 to 120	14 to 18	½ (for seed); bury roots of plants.	When peppers are 2 to 3 inches in diameter (depends on variety).

Comment: Require hot weather. If you start your own seeds indoors, plant 5 or 6 weeks before transplanting time. Cover container for a few days after planting to keep soil moist. Start indoors if possible. Allow one plant per 1-gallon container.

Plant	Light	When to plant	Days from seed to harvest	Space between plants (inches)	Planting depth (inches)	When to harvest
RADISHES (mild)	Do well in partial shade.	2 to 4 weeks before frost-free date.	25 to 35	1	½	When ½ to 1 inch in diameter.

Comment: Cannot withstand heat. The faster they grow, the better the quality. Be sure they get fertilizer at seeding time. Radishes are at their best for only a few days, so you may wish to make several plantings at 1-week intervals. You may also want to try the hotter, large, winter radishes, which need 75 days or more growing time and are planted to mature just before fall frost.

Plant	Light	When to plant	Days from seed to harvest	Space between plants (inches)	Planting depth (inches)	When to harvest
SUMMER SQUASH	Does best in full sunlight.	On frost-free date.	50 to 60	One plant per 5-gallon container.	1 to 2	Depends on variety; see your seed package.

Comment: Plant the bush types of this vegetable.

Plant	Light	When to plant	Days from seed to harvest	Space between plants (inches)	Planting depth (inches)	When to harvest
SWISS CHARD	Tolerates partial shade.	2 to 4 weeks before frost-free date.	30 to 40	4 to 5	½	When leaves are 3 inches or more in length.

Comment: Only one planting is necessary; new leaves replace the harvested leaves. Outer leaves may be harvested without injuring the plant. Each seed cluster contains several seeds.

Plant	Light	When to plant	Days from seed to harvest	Space between plants (inches)	Planting depth (inches)	When to harvest
TOMATOES	Require full sunlight.	Transplant on frost-free date (start seeds 5 to 7 weeks before transplanting).	55 to 100	One plant per 1- to 3-gallon container.	½ (for seed); bury roots of plants.	When tomatoes turn pink or almost red.

Comment: Dwarf tomatoes offer a large return for a small space. They need warm weather. The Tiny Tim and other dwarf varieties do well in containers.

Plant	Light	When to plant	Days from seed to harvest	Space between plants (inches)	Planting depth (inches)	When to harvest
TURNIPS	Tolerate partial shade.	4 to 6 weeks before frost-free date and 6 to 8 weeks before first fall freeze.	30 to 80 (30 days for greens).	3 to 4, when harvesting for greens.	½	Thin when large enough to make greens; leave others to mature (2 inches or more in diameter).

Comment: Turnips are a cool-season vegetable.

Ornamental Vegetables

If you want to grow ornamental vegetables, there are several attractive varieties that are pretty as well as tasty. Here are a few suggestions.

Salad Bowl Lettuce produces many curled, wavy, bright-green leaves. If you want color in your lettuce, grow the **Ruby** variety. This is a beautiful, nonheading salad lettuce with fancy, frilled leaves that are a bright red.

Another bright-red vegetable is a swiss chard variety called **Rhubarb**. It looks like rhubarb and is easy to grow.

A kale variety called **Flowering Kale from the Orient** has bright red and green leaves.

All tomato varieties are decorative. **Tiny Tim,** a miniature tomato, is an especially colorful plant that adds color and taste to any salad.

CANNING

Canning Your Home Grown Fruits and Vegetables

Organisms that cause food spoilage—molds, yeasts, and bacteria—are always present in the air, water, and soil. Enzymes that may cause undesirable changes in flavor, color, and texture are present in raw fruits and vegetables.

When you can fruits and vegetables you heat them hot enough and long enough to destroy spoilage organisms. This heating (or processing) also stops the action of enzymes. Processing is done in either a boiling-water-bath canner or a steam-pressure canner. The kind of canner that should be used depends on the kind of food being canned.

THE RIGHT CANNER FOR EACH FOOD

Fruits, tomatoes, and pickled vegetables: use a boiling-water-bath canner. You can process these acid foods safely in boiling water.

Vegetables except tomatoes: use a steam-pressure canner. To process these low-acid foods safely in a reasonable length of time takes a temperature higher than that of boiling water.

A pressure saucepan equipped with an accurate indicator or gauge for controlling pressures at 10 pounds (240° F.) may be used as a steam-pressure canner for vegetables in pint jars or No. 2 tin cans. If you use a pressure saucepan, add 20 minutes to the processing times given for each vegetable.

GETTING YOUR EQUIPMENT READY

Steam-Pressure Canner

For the safe operation of your canner, clean petcock and safety-valve openings by drawing a string or narrow strip of cloth through them. Do this at the beginning of the canning season and often during the season.

Check your pressure gauge. An accurate pressure gauge is necessary to get the processing temperatures needed to make food keep.

A weighted gauge needs to be thoroughly clean.

A dial gauge, old or new, should be checked before the canning season, and also during the season, if you use the canner often. Ask your county home demonstration agent, dealer, or manufacturer about checking it.

If your gauge is off 5 pounds or more, you'd better get a new one. But if the gauge is not more than 4 pounds off, you can correct for it as shown below. As a reminder, tie a tag on the canner stating the reading to use to get the correct pressure. The food should be processed at 10 pounds steam pressure.

If the gauge reads high:
1 pound high—process at 11 pounds.
2 pounds high—process at 12 pounds.
3 pounds high—process at 13 pounds.
4 pounds high—process at 14 pounds.

If the gauge reads low:
1 pound low—process at 9 pounds.
2 pounds low—process at 8 pounds.
3 pounds low—process at 7 pounds.
4 pounds low—process at 6 pounds.

Have canner thoroughly clean. Wash canner kettle well if you have not used it for some time. Don't put the cover in water—wipe it with a soapy cloth, then with a damp, clean cloth. Dry well.

Water-Bath Canner

Water-bath canners are available on the market. Any big metal container may be used as a boiling-water-bath canner if it is deep enough so that the water is well over the tops of jars and has space to boil freely. Allow 2 to 4 inches above jar tops for brisk boiling. The canner must have a tight-fitting cover and a wire or wooden rack. If the rack has dividers, jars will not touch each other or fall against the sides of the canner during processing.

If a steam-pressure canner is deep enough, you can use it for a water bath. Cover, but do not fasten. Leave petcock wide open, so that steam escapes and pressure does not build up inside the canner.

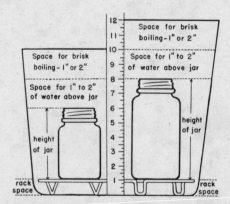

Glass Jars

Be sure all jars and closures are perfect. Discard any with cracks, chips, dents, or rust; defects prevent airtight seals.

Select the size of closure—widemouth or regular—that fits your jars.

Wash glass jars in hot, soapy water and rinse well. Wash and rinse all lids and bands. Metal lids with sealing compound may need boiling or holding in boiling water for a few minutes—follow the manufacturer's directions.

If you use rubber rings, have clean, new rings of the right size for the jars. Don't test by stretching. Wash rings in hot, soapy water and rinse well.

Tin Cans

Select desired type and size. Three types of tin cans are used in home canning—plain tin, C-enamel (corn enamel), and R-enamel (sanitary or standard enamel). For most products plain tin cans are satisfactory. Enameled cans are recommended for certain fruits and vegetables to prevent discoloration of food, but they are not necessary for a wholesome product. The types of cans and the foods for which they are recommended are:

C-enamel:	Corn
R-enamel:	Beets, red berries, red or black cherries, plums, pumpkin, rhubarb, winter squash.
Plain:	All other fruits and vegetables for which canning directions are given.

Directions are given for canning most fruits and vegetables in No. 2 and No. 2½ tin cans. A No. 2 can holds about 2½ cups, and a No. 2½ can about 3½ cups.

Use only cans in good condition: See that cans, lids, and gaskets are perfect. Discard badly bent, dented, or rusted cans, and lids with damaged gaskets. Keep lids in paper packing until ready to use. The paper protects the lids from dirt and moisture.

Wash cans: Just before use, wash cans in clean water; drain upside down. Do not wash lids; washing may damage the gaskets. If lids are dusty or dirty, rinse with clean water or wipe with a damp cloth just before you put them on the cans.

Check the sealer: Make sure the sealer you use is properly adjusted. To test, put a little water into a can, seal it, then submerge the can

A can sealer is needed if tin cans are used.

in boiling water for a few seconds. If air bubbles rise from around the can, the seam is not right. Adjust sealer, following manufacturer's directions.

GENERAL CANNING PROCEDURE

Selecting Fruits and Vegetables for Canning

Choose fresh, firm fruits and young, tender vegetables. Can them before they lose their freshness. If you must hold them, keep them in a cool, airy place. If you buy fruits and vegetables to can, try to get them from a nearby garden or orchard.

For best quality in the canned product, use only perfect fruits and vegetables. Sort them for size and ripeness; they cook more evenly that way.

Washing

Wash all fruits and vegetables thoroughly, whether or not they are to be pared. Dirt contains some of the bacteria hardest to kill. Wash small lots at a time, under running water or through several changes of water. Lift the food out of the water each time so dirt that has been washed off won't go back on the food. Rinse pan thoroughly between washings. Don't let fruits or vegetables soak; they may lose flavor and food value. Handle them gently to avoid bruising.

Filling Containers

Raw pack or hot pack: Fruits and vegetables may be packed raw into glass jars or tin cans or

preheated and packed hot. Directions for both raw and hot packs are given for most of the foods.

Most raw fruits and vegetables should be packed tightly into the container because they shrink during processing; a few—like corn, lima beans, and peas—should be packed loosely because they expand.

Hot food should be packed fairly loosely. It should be at or near boiling temperature when it is packed.

There should be enough syrup, water, or juice to fill in around the solid food in the container and to cover the food. Food at the top of the container tends to darken if not covered with liquid. It takes from ½ to 1½ cups of liquid for a quart glass jar or a No. 2½ tin can.

Head space: With only a few exceptions, some space should be left between the packed food and the closure. The amount of space to allow at the top of the jar or can is given in the detailed directions for canning each food.

Closing Glass Jars

Closures for glass jars are of two main types. Metal screwband and flat metal lid with sealing compound: To use this type, wipe jar rim clean after produce is packed. Put lid on, with sealing compound next to glass. Screw metal band down tight by hand. When band is tight, this lid has enough give to let air escape during processing. Do not tighten screw band further after taking jar from canner.

Screw bands that are in good condition may be reused. You may remove bands as soon as jars are cool. Metal lids with sealing compound may be used only once.

Porcelain-lined zinc cap with shoulder rubber ring: Fit wet rubber ring down on jar shoulder, but don't stretch unnecessarily. Fill jar; wipe rubber ring and jar rim clean. Then screw cap down firmly and turn it back ¼ inch. As soon as you take jar from canner, screw cap down tight, to complete seal.

Porcelain-lined zinc caps may be reused as long as they are in good condition. Rubber rings should not be reused.

Exhausting and Sealing Tin Cans

Tin cans are sealed before processing. The temperature of the food in the cans must be 170° F. or higher when the cans are sealed. Food is heated to this temperature to drive out air so that there will be a good vacuum in the can after processing and cooling. Removal of air also helps prevent discoloring of canned food and change in flavor.

Food packed raw must be heated in the cans (exhausted) before the cans are sealed. Food packed hot may be sealed without further heating if you are sure the temperature of the food has not dropped below 170° F. To make sure, test with a thermometer, placing the bulb at the center of the can. If the thermometer registers lower than 170°, or if you do not make this test, exhaust the cans.

To exhaust, place open, filled cans on a rack in a kettle in which there is enough boiling water to come to about 2 inches below the tops of the cans. Cover the kettle. Bring water back to boiling. Boil until a thermometer inserted at the center of the can registers 170° F.—or for the length of time given in the directions for the fruit or vegetables you are canning.

Remove cans from the water one at a time, and add boiling packing liquid or water if necessary to bring head space back to the level specified for each product. Place clean lid on filled can. Seal at once.

Processing

Process fruits, tomatoes, and pickled vegetables in a boiling-water-bath canner according to the directions given. Process vegetables in a steam-pressure canner according to the directions given.

Cooling Canned Food

Glass jars: As you take jars from the canner, complete seals at once if necessary. If liquid boiled out in processing, do not open jar to add more. Seal the jar just as it is.

Cool jars top side up. Give each jar enough room to let air get at all sides. Never set a hot jar on a cold surface; instead set the jars on a

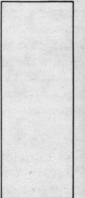

Cool jars top side up on a rack, leaving space between jars so air can circulate.

Cool tin cans in cold water; change water frequently to cool cans quickly.

rack or on a folded cloth. Keep hot jars away from drafts, but don't slow cooling by covering them.

Tin cans: Put tin cans in cold, clean water to cool them; change water as needed to cool cans quickly. Take cans out of the water while they are still warm so they will dry in the air. If you stack cans, stagger them so that air can get around them.

Day-After-Canning Jobs

Test the seal on glass jars with porcelain-lined caps by turning each jar partly over in your hands. To test a jar that has a flat metal lid, press center of lid; if lid is down and will not move, jar is sealed. Or tap the center of the lid with a spoon. A clear, ringing sound means a good seal. A dull note does not always mean a poor seal; store jars without leaks and check for spoilage before use.

If you find a leaky jar, use unspoiled food right away. Or can it again; empty the jar, and pack and process food as if it were fresh. Before using jar or lid again check for defects.

When jars are thoroughly cool, take off the screw bands carefully. If a band sticks, covering for a moment with a hot, damp cloth may help loosen it.

Before storing canned food, wipe containers clean. Label to show contents, date, and lot number—if you canned more than one lot in a day. Wash bands; store them in a dry place.

Label jars after they have been cooled.

Storing Canned Food

Properly canned food stored in a cool, dry place will retain good eating quality for a year. Canned food stored in a warm place near hot pipes, a range, or a furnace, or indirect sunlight may lose some of its eating quality in a few weeks or months, depending on the temperature.

Dampness may corrode cans or metal lids and cause leakage so the food will spoil.

Freezing does not cause food spoilage unless the seal is damaged or the jar is broken. However, frozen canned food may be less palatable than properly stored canned food. In an unheated storage place it is well to protect canned food by wrapping the jars in paper or covering them with a blanket.

On Guard Against Spoilage

Don't use canned food that shows any sign of spoilage. Look closely at each container before opening it. Bulging can ends, jar lids, or rings, or a leak—these may mean the seal has broken and the food has spoiled. When you open a container look for other signs—spurting liquid, an off odor, or mold.

It's possible for canned vegetables to contain the poison causing botulism—a serious food poisoning—without showing signs of spoilage. To avoid any risk of botulism, it is essential that the pressure canner be in perfect order and that every canning recommendation be followed exactly. Unless you're absolutely sure of your gauge and canning methods, boil home-canned vegetables before tasting. Heating usually makes any odor of spoilage more evident.

Bring vegetables to a rolling boil; then cover and boil for at least 10 minutes. Boil spinach and corn 20 minutes. If the food looks spoiled, foams, or has an off odor during heating, destroy it. Burn spoiled vegetables, or dispose of the food so that it will not be eaten by humans or animals.

HOW TO CAN FRUITS, TOMATOES, PICKLED VEGETABLES

Fruits, tomatoes, and pickled vegetables are canned according to the general directions already given. Detailed directions for each food follow and the special directions given below apply only to acid foods.

Points on Packing

Raw pack: Put cold, raw fruits into container and cover with boiling-hot syrup, juice or water. Press tomatoes down in the containers so they are covered with their own juice; add no liquid.

Hot pack: Heat fruits in syrup, in water or steam, or in extracted juice before packing. Juicy fruits and tomatoes may be preheated without added liquid and packed in the juice that cooks out.

To hot pack fruit, pack heated fruit loosely into jars.

Cover fruit with boiling liquid before closing jar and processing in boiling-water bath.

Sweetening Fruit

Sugar helps canned fruit hold its shape, color, and flavor. Directions for canning most fruits call for sweetening to be added in the form of sugar syrup. For very juicy fruit packed hot, use sugar without added liquid.

To make sugar syrup: Mix sugar with water or with juice extracted from some of the fruit. Use a thin, medium, or heavy syrup to suit the sweetness of the fruit and your taste. To make syrup, combine:

4 cups of water or juice

2 cups sugar	For 5 cups THIN syrup.
3 cups sugar	For 5½ cups MEDIUM syrup
4¾ cups sugar	For 6½ cups HEAVY syrup.

Heat sugar and water or juice together until sugar is dissolved. Skim if necessary.

To extract juice: Crush thoroughly ripe, sound juicy fruit. Heat to simmering (185° to 210° F.) over low heat. Strain through jelly bag or other cloth.

To add sugar directly to fruit: For juicy fruit to be packed hot, add about ½ cup sugar to each quart of raw, prepared fruit. Heat to simmering (185° to 210° F.) over low heat. Pack fruit in the juice that cooks out.

To add sweetening other than sugar: You can use light corn syrup or mild-flavored honey to replace as much as half the sugar called for in canning fruit. Do not use brown sugar, or molasses, sorghum, or other strong-flavored syrups; their flavor overpowers the fruit flavor and they may darken the fruit.

Canning Unsweetened Fruit

You may can fruit without sweetening—in its own juice, in extracted juice, or in water. Sugar is not needed to prevent spoilage; processing is the same for unsweetened fruit as for sweetened.

Processing in Boiling-Water Bath

Directions: Put filled glass jars or tin cans into canner containing hot or boiling water. For raw pack in glass jars have water in canner hot but not boiling; for all other packs have water boiling.

Add boiling water if needed to bring water an inch or two over tops of containers; don't pour boiling water directly on glass jars. Put cover on canner.

When water in canner comes to a rolling boil,

start to count processing time. Boil gently and steadily for time recommended for the food you are canning. Add boiling water during processing if needed to keep containers covered.

Remove containers from the canner immediately when processing time is up.

Processing times: Follow timing carefully. The times given apply only when a specific food is prepared according to detailed directions. If you live at an altitude of 1,000 feet or more, you have to add to these processing times in canning directions, as follows:

DIRECTIONS FOR FRUITS, TOMATOES, PICKLED VEGETABLES

Apples

Pare and core apples; cut in pieces. To keep fruit from darkening, drop pieces into water containing 2 tablespoons each of salt and vinegar per gallon. Drain, then boil 5 minutes in thin syrup or water.

In glass jars: Pack hot fruit to ½ inch of top. Cover with hot syrup or water, leaving ½-inch space at top of jar. Adjust jar lids. Process in

Altitude	Increase in processing time if the time called for is—	
	20 minutes or less	More than 20 minutes
1,000 feet	1 minute	2 minutes.
2,000 feet	2 minutes	4 minutes.
3,000 feet	3 minutes	6 minutes.
4,000 feet	4 minutes	8 minutes.
5,000 feet	5 minutes	10 minutes.
6,000 feet	6 minutes	12 minutes.
7,000 feet	7 minutes	14 minutes.
8,000 feet	8 minutes	16 minutes.
9,000 feet	9 minutes	18 minutes.
10,000 feet	10 minutes	20 minutes.

To Figure Yield of Canned Fruit From Fresh

The number of quarts of canned food you can get from a given quantity of fresh fruit depends upon the quality, variety, maturity, and size of the fruit, whether it is whole, in halves, or in slices, and whether it is packed raw or hot.

Generally, the following amounts of fresh fruit or tomatoes (as purchased or picked) make 1 quart of canned food:

	Pounds
Apples	2½ to 3
Berries, except strawberries	1½ to 3 (1 to 2 quart boxes)
Cherries (canned unpitted)	2 to 2½
Peaches	2 to 3
Pears	2 to 3
Plums	1½ to 2½
Tomatoes	2½ to 3½

In 1 pound there are about 3 medium apples and pears; 4 medium peaches or tomatoes; 8 medium plums.

boiling-water bath (212° F.).

| Pint jars | 15 minutes |
| Quart Jars | 20 minutes |

As soon as you remove jars from canner, complete seals if necessary.

In tin cans: Pack hot fruit to ¼ inch of top. Fill to top with hot syrup or water. Exhaust to 170° F. (about 10 minutes) and seal cans. Process in boiling-water bath (212° F.).

| No. 2 cans | 10 minutes |
| No. 2½ cans | 10 minutes |

Applesauce

Make applesauce, sweetened or unsweetened. Heat to simmering (185°-210° F.); stir to keep it from sticking.

In glass jars: Pack hot applesauce to ¼ inch of top. Adjust lids. Process in boiling-water bath (212° F.).

| Pint jars | 10 minutes |
| Quart jars | 10 minutes |

As soon as you remove jars from canner, complete seals if necessary.

In tin cans: Pack hot applesauce to top. Exhaust to 170° F. (about 10 minutes) and seal cans. Process in boiling-water bath (212° F.).

No. 2 cans	10 minutes
No. 2½ cans	10 minutes

Apricots

Follow method for peaches. Peeling may be omitted.

Beets, Pickled

Cut off beet tops, leaving 1 inch of stem. Also leave root. Wash beets, cover with boiling water, and cook until tender. Remove skins and slice beets. For pickling syrup, use 2 cups vinegar (or 1½ cups vinegar and ½ cup water) to 2 cups sugar. Heat to boiling.

Pack beets in glass jars to ½ inch of top. Add ½ teaspoon salt to pints, 1 teaspoon to quarts. Cover with boiling syrup, leaving ½-inch space at top of jar. Adjust jar lids. Process in boiling-water bath (212° F.).

Pint jars	30 minutes
Quart Jars	30 minutes

As soon as you remove jars from canner, complete seals if necessary.

Berries, Except Strawberries

Raw Pack: Wash berries; drain.

In glass jars: Fill jars to ½ inch of top. For a full pack, shake berries down while filling jars. Cover with boiling syrup, leaving ½-inch space at top. Adjust lids. Process in boiling-water bath (212° F.).

Pint jars	10 minutes
Quart jars	15 minutes

As soon as you remove jars from canner, complete seal if necessary.

In tin cans: Fill cans to ¼ inch of top. For a full pack, shake berries down while filling cans. Fill to top with boiling syrup. Exhaust to 170° F. (10 minutes); seal cans. Process in boiling-water bath (212° F.).

No. 2 cans	15 minutes
No. 2½ cans	20 minutes

Hot Pack: (For firm berries.) Wash berries and drain well. Add ½ cup sugar to each quart fruit. Cover pan and bring to boil; shake pan to keep berries from sticking.

In glass jars: Pack hot berries to ½ inch of top. Adjust jar lids. Process in boiling-water bath (212° F.).

Pint jars	10 minutes
Quart jars	15 minutes

As soon as you remove jars from canner, complete seals if necessary.

In tin cans: Pack hot berries to top. Exhaust to 170° F. (about 10 minutes) and seal cans. Process in boiling-water bath (212° F.).

No. 2 cans	15 minutes
No. 2½ cans	20 minutes

Cherries

Raw Pack: Wash cherries; remove pits, if desired.

In glass jars: Fill jars to ½ inch to top. For a full pack, shake cherries down while filling jars. Cover with boiling syrup, leaving ½-inch space at top. Adjust lids. Process in boiling-water bath (212° F.).

Pint jars	20 minutes
Quart jars	25 minutes

As soon as you remove jars from canner, complete seals if necessary.

In tin cans: Fill cans to ¼ inch of top. For a full pack, shake cherries down while filling cans. Fill to top with boiling syrup. Exhaust to 170° F. (about 10 minutes) and seal cans. Process in boiling-water bath (212° F.).

No. 2 cans	20 minutes
No. 2½ cans	25 minutes

Hot Pack: Wash cherries; remove pits, if desired. Add ½ cup sugar to each quart of fruit. Add a little water to unpitted cherries to keep them from sticking while heating. Cover pan and bring to a boil.

In glass jars: Pack hot to ½ inch of top. Adjust jar lids. Process in boiling-water bath (212° F.).

Pint jars	10 minutes
Quart jars	15 minutes

As soon as you remove jars from canner, complete seals if necessary.

In tin cans: Pack hot to top of cans. Exhaust to 170° F. (about 10 minutes) and seal cans. Process in boiling-water bath (212° F.).

No. 2 cans	15 minutes
No. 2½ cans	20 minutes

Fruit Juices

Wash: remove pits, if desired, and crush fruit. Heat to simmering (185°-210° F.). Strain through cloth bag. Add sugar, if desired—about 1 cup to 1 gallon juice. Reheat to simmering.

In glass jars: Fill jars to ½ inch of top with hot juice. Adjust lids. Process in boiling-water bath (212° F.).

Pint jars   5 minutes
Quart jars   5 minutes

As soon as you remove jars from canner, complete seals if necessary.

In tin cans: Fill cans to top with hot juice. Seal at once. Process in boiling-water bath (212° F.).

No. 2 cans   5 minutes
No. 2½ cans   5 minutes

Fruit Purees

Use sound, ripe fruit. Wash; remove pits, if desired. Cut large fruit in pieces. Simmer until soft; add a little water if needed to keep fruit from sticking. Put through a strainer or food mill. Add sugar to taste. Heat again to simmering (185°-210° F.).

In glass jars: Pack hot to ½ inch of top. Adjust lids. Process in boiling-water bath (212° F.).

Pint jars   10 minutes
Quart jars   10 minutes

As soon as you remove jars from canner, complete seals if necessary.

In tin cans: Pack hot to top. Exhaust to 170° F. (about 10 minutes), and seal cans. Process in boiling-water bath (212° F.).

No. 2 cans   10 minutes
No. 2½ cans   10 minutes

Peaches

Wash peaches and remove skins. Dipping the fruit in boiling water, then quickly in cold water makes peeling easier. Cut peaches in halves; remove pits. Slice if desired. To prevent fruit from darkening during preparation, drop it into water containing 2 tablespoons each of salt and vinegar per gallon. Drain just before heating or packing raw.

Raw Pack: Prepare peaches as directed above.

In glass jars: Pack raw fruit to ½ inch of top. Cover with boiling syrup, leaving ½-inch space at top of jar. Adjust jar lids. Process in boiling-water bath (212° F.).

Pint jars   25 minutes
Quart jars   30 minutes

As soon as you remove jars from canner, complete seals if necessary.

In tin cans: Pack raw fruit to ¼ inch of top. Fill to top with boiling syrup. Exhaust to 170° F. (about 10 minutes) and seal cans. Process in boiling-water bath (212° F.).

No. 2 cans   30 minutes
No. 2½ cans   35 minutes

Hot Pack: Prepare peaches as directed above. Heat peaches through in hot syrup. If fruit is very juicy you may heat it with sugar, adding no liquid.

In glass jars: Pack hot fruit to ½ inch of top. Cover with boiling liquid, leaving ½-inch space at top of jar. Adjust jar lids. Process in boiling-water bath (212° F.).

Pint jars   20 minutes
Quart jars   25 minutes

As soon as you remove jars from canner, complete seals if necessary.

In tin cans: Pack hot fruit to ¼ inch of top. Fill to top with boiling liquid. Exhaust to 170° F. (about 10 minutes) and seal cans. Process in boiling-water bath (212° F.).

No. 2 cans   25 minutes
No. 2½ cans   30 minutes

Peaches can be peeled easily if they are dipped in boiling water, then in cold water.

Pears

Wash pears. Peel, cut in halves, and core. Continue as with peaches, either raw pack or hot pack.

Plums

Wash plums. To can whole, prick skins. Freestone varieties may be halved and pitted.

Raw Pack: Prepare plums as directed above.

In glass jars: Pack raw fruit to ½ inch of top. Cover with boiling syrup, leaving ½-inch space at top of jar. Adjust jar lids. Process in boiling-water bath (212° F.).

Pint jars   20 minutes
Quart jars   25 minutes

As soon as you remove jars from canner, complete seals if necessary.

In tin cans: Pack raw fruit to ¼ inch of top. Fill to top with boiling syrup. Exhaust to 170° F. (about 10 minutes) and seal cans. Process in boiling-water bath (212° F.).

No. 2 cans   15 minutes
No. 2½ cans   20 minutes

Hot Pack: Prepare plums as directed above. Heat to boiling in syrup or juice. If fruit is very juicy you may heat it with sugar, adding no liquid.

In glass jars: Pack hot fruit to ½ inch of top. Cover with boiling liquid, leaving ½-inch space at top of jar. Adjust jar lids. Process in boiling-water bath (212° F.).

Pint jars   20 minutes
Quart jars   25 minutes

As soon as you remove jars from canner, complete seals if necessary.

In tin cans: Pack hot fruit to ¼ inch of top. Fill to top with boiling liquid. Exhaust to 170° F. (about 10 minutes) and seal cans. Process in boiling-water bath (212° F.).

No. 2 cans   15 minutes
No. 2½ cans   20 minutes

Rhubarb

Wash rhubarb and cut into ½-inch pieces. Add ½ cup sugar to each quart rhubarb and let stand to draw out juice. Bring to boiling.

In glass jars: Pack hot to ½ inch of top. Adjust lids. Process in boiling-water bath (212° F.).

Pint jars   10 minutes
Quart jars   10 minutes

As soon as you remove jars from canner, complete seals if necessary.

In tin cans: Pack hot to top of cans. Exhaust to 170° F. (about 10 minutes) and seal cans. Process in boiling-water bath (212° F.).

No. 2 cans   10 minutes
No. 2½ cans   10 minutes

Tomatoes

Use only firm, ripe tomatoes. To loosen skins, dip into boiling water for about ½ minute; then dip quickly into cold water. Cut out stem ends and peel tomatoes.

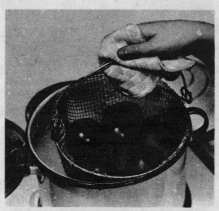

To peel tomatoes, dip them in boiling water, then quickly in cold water to loosen skins.

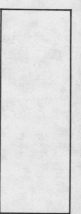

To raw pack tomatoes, put peeled tomatoes in jars and press down to fill spaces.

Raw Pack: Leave tomatoes whole or cut in halves or quarters.

In glass jars: Pack tomatoes to ½ inch of top, pressing gently to fill spaces. Add no water. Add ½ teaspoon salt to pints; 1 teaspoon to quarts. Adjust lids. Process in boiling-water bath (212° F.).

Pint jars   35 minutes
Quart jars   45 minutes

As soon as you remove jars from canner, complete seals if necessary.

In tin cans: Pack tomatoes to top of cans, pressing gently to fill spaces. Add no water. Add ½ teaspoon salt to No. 2 cans; 1 teaspoon to No. 2½ cans. Exhaust to 170° F., (about 15 minutes) and seal cans. Process in boiling-water bath (212° F.).

No. 2 cans   45 minutes
No. 2½ cans   55 minutes

Hot Pack: Quarter peeled tomatoes. Bring to boil; stir to keep tomatoes from sticking.

In glass jars: Pack boiling-hot tomatoes to ½ inch of top. Add ½ teaspoon salt to pints; 1 teaspoon to quarts. Adjust jar lids. Process in boiling-water bath (212° F.).

Pint jars   10 minutes
Quart jars   10 minutes

As soon as you remove jars from canner, complete seals if necessary.

In tin cans: Pack boiling-hot tomatoes to ¼ inch of top. Add no water. Add ½ teaspoon salt to No. 2 cans; 1 teaspoon to No. 2½ cans. Exhaust to 170° F. (about 10 minutes) and seal cans. Process in boiling-water bath (212° F.).

No. 2 cans   10 minutes
No. 2½ cans   10 minutes

Tomato Juice

Use ripe, juicy tomatoes. Wash, remove stem ends, cut into pieces. Simmer until softened, stirring often. Put through strainer. Add 1 teaspoon salt to each quart juice. Reheat at once just to boiling.

In glass jars: Fill jars with boiling-hot juice to ½ inch of top. Adjust jar lids. Process in boiling-water bath (212° F.).

Pint jars   10 minutes
Quart jars   10 minutes

As soon as you remove jars from canner, complete seals if necessary.

In tin cans: Fill cans to top with boiling-hot juice. Seal cans at once. Process in boiling-water bath (212° F.).

No. 2 Cans   15 minutes
No. 2½ cans   15 minutes

HOW TO CAN VEGETABLES

Can vegetables according to general directions already given. Detailed directions for each vegetable follow and special directions below apply only to vegetables.

Points on Packing

Raw pack: Pack cold raw vegetables (except corn, lima beans, and peas) tightly into con-

tainer and cover with boiling water.

Hot pack: Preheat vegetables in water or steam. Cover with cooking liquid or boiling water. Cooking liquid is recommended for packing most vegetables because it may contain minerals and vitamins dissolved out of the food. Boiling water is recommended when cooking liquid is dark, gritty, or strong-flavored, and when there isn't enough cooking liquid.

Processing in a Pressure Canner

Use a steam-pressure canner for processing all vegetables except tomatoes and pickled vegetables. A pressure saucepan may be used for pint jars and No. 2 cans.

Directions: Follow the manufacturer's directions for the canner you are using. Here are a few pointers on the use of any steam-pressure canner:

Put 2 or 3 inches of boiling water in the bottom of the canner; the amount of water to use depends on the size and shape of the canner.

Set filled glass jars or tin cans on a rack in the canner so that steam can flow around each container. If two layers of cans or jars are put in, stagger the second layer. Use a rack between layers of glass jars.

Fasten canner cover securely so that no steam can escape except through vent (petcock or weighted-gauge opening).

Watch until steam pours steadily from vent. Let it escape for 10 minutes or more to drive all air from the canner. Then close petcock or put on weighted gauge.

Let pressure rise to 10 pounds (240° F.). The moment this pressure is reached start counting processing time. Keep pressure constant by regulating heat under the canner. Do not lower pressure by opening petcock. Keep drafts from blowing on canner.

When processing time is up, remove canner from heat immediately.

With glass jars, let canner stand until pressure is zero. Never try to rush the cooling by pouring cold water over the canner. When pressure registers zero, wait a minute or two, then slowly open petcock or take off weighted gauge. Unfasten cover and tilt the far side up so steam escapes away from you. Take jars from canner.

With tin cans, release steam in canner as soon as canner is removed from heat by opening pet-

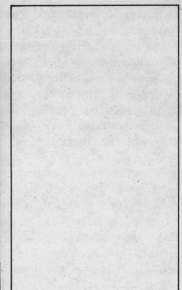

To process vegetables, bring pressure in canner up to 10 pounds, then start to count processing time.

cock or taking off weighted gauge. Then take off canner cover and remove cans.

Processing times: Follow processing times carefully. The times given apply only when a specific food is prepared according to detailed directions.

If you live at an altitude of less than 2,000 feet above sea level, process vegetables at 10 pounds pressure for the times given.

At altitudes above sea level, it takes more than 10 pounds pressure to reach 240° F. If you live at an altitude of 2,000 feet, process vegetables at 11 pounds pressure. At 4,000 feet, use 12 pounds pressure; at 6,000 feet, 13 pounds pressure; at 8,000 feet, 14 pounds pressure; at 10,000 feet, 15 pounds pressure.

A weighted gauge may need to be corrected for altitude by the manufacturer.

Yield of Canned Vegetables From Fresh

The number of quarts of canned food you can get from a given amount of fresh vegetables depends on quality, condition, maturity, and variety of the vegetable, size of pieces, and on the way the vegetable is packed—raw or hot pack.

Generally, the following amounts of fresh vegetables (as purchased or picked) make 1 quart of canned food:

	Pounds
Asparagus	2½ to 4½
Beans	3 to 5
Beans, snap	1½ to 2½
Beets, without tops	2 to 3½
Carrots, without tops	2 to 3
Corn, sweet, in husks	3 to 6
Okra	1½
Peas, green, in pods	3 to 6
Pumpkin or winter squash	1½ to 3
Spinach and other greens	2 to 6
Squash, summer	2 to 4
Sweetpotatoes	2 to 3

Directions for Vegetables

Asparagus

Raw Pack: Wash asparagus; trim off scales and tough ends and wash again. Cut into 1-inch pieces.

In glass jars: Pack asparagus as tightly as possible without crushing to ½ inch of top. Add ½ teaspoon salt to pints; 1 teaspoon to quarts. Cover with boiling water, leaving ½-inch space at top of jar. Adjust jar lids. Process in pressure canner at 10 pounds pressure (240° F.).

Pint jars	25 minutes
Quart jars	30 minutes

As soon as you remove jars from canner, complete seals if necessary.

In tin cans: Pack asparagus as tightly as possible without crushing to ¼ inch of top. Add ½ teaspoon salt to No. 2 cans; 1 teaspoon to No. 2½ cans. Fill to top with boiling water. Exhaust to 170° F. (about 10 minutes) and seal cans. Process in pressure canner at 10 pounds pressure (240° F.).

No. 2 cans	20 minutes
No. 2½ cans	20 minutes

Hot Pack: Wash asparagus; trim off scales and tough ends and wash again. Cut in 1-inch pieces; cover with boiling water. Boil 2 or 3 minutes.

In glass jars: Pack hot asparagus loosely to ½ inch of top. Add ½ teaspoon salt to pints; 1 teaspoon to quarts. Cover with boiling-hot cooking liquid, or if liquid contains grit use boiling water. Leave ½-inch space at top of jar. Adjust jar lids. Process in pressure canner at 10 pounds pressure (240° F.).

Pint jars	25 minutes
Quart jars	30 minutes

As soon as you remove jars from canner, complete seals if necessary.

In tin cans: Pack hot asparagus loosely to ¼ inch of top. Add ½ teaspoon salt to No. 2 cans; 1 teaspoon to No. 2½ cans. Fill to top with boiling-hot cooking liquid, or if liquid contains grit use boiling water. Exhaust to 170° F. (about 10 minutes) and seal cans. Process in pressure canner at 10 pounds pressure (240° F.).

No. 2 cans	20 minutes
No. 2½ cans	20 minutes

Beans, Dry, With Tomato or Molasses Sauce

Sort and wash dry beans (kidney, navy, or yellow eye). Cover with boiling water; boil 2 minutes, remove from heat and let soak 1 hour. Heat to boiling, drain, and save liquid for making sauce.

In glass jars: Fill jars three-fourths full with hot beans. Add a small piece of salt pork, ham, or bacon. Fill to 1 inch of top with hot sauce (see recipes below). Adjust jar lids. Process in pressure canner at 10 pounds pressure (240° F.)

Pint jars	65 minutes
Quart jars	75 minutes

As soon as you remove jars from canner, complete seals if necessary.

In tin cans: Fill cans three-fourths full with hot beans. Add a small piece of salt pork, ham, or bacon. Fill to ¼ inch of top with hot sauce (see recipes below). Exhaust to 170° F. (about 20 minutes) and seal cans. Process in pressure canner at 10 pounds pressure (240° F.).

No. 2 cans	65 minutes
No. 2½ cans	75 minutes

Tomato sauce: Mix 1 quart tomato juice, 3 tablespoons sugar, 2 teaspoons salt, 1 tablespoon chopped onion, and ¼ teaspoon mixture of ground cloves, allspice, mace, and cayenne. Heat to boiling.

Or mix 1 cup tomato catsup with 3 cups of water or soaking liquid from beans and heat to boiling.

Molasses sauce: Mix 1 quart water or soaking liquid from beans, 3 tablespoons dark molasses, 1 tablespoon vinegar, 2 teaspoons salt, and ¾ teaspoon powdered dry mustard. Heat to boiling.

Beans, Dry, Baked

Soak and boil beans according to directions for beans with sauce.

Place small pieces of salt pork, ham, or bacon in earthenware crock or a pan.

Add beans. Add enough molasses sauce to cover beans. Cover crock and bake 4 to 5 hours at 350° F. (moderate oven). Add water as needed—about every hour.

In glass jars: Pack hot beans to 1 inch of top. Adjust jar lids. Process in pressure canner at 10 pounds pressure (240° F.).

Pint jars	80 minutes
Quart jars	100 minutes

As soon as you remove jars from canner, complete seals if necessary.

In tin cans: Pack hot beans to ¼ inch of top. Exhaust to 170° F. (about 15 minutes) and seal cans. Process in pressure canner at 10 pounds pressure (240° F.).

No. 2 cans	95 minutes
No. 2½ cans	115 minutes

Beans, Fresh Lima

Can only young, tender beans.

Raw Pack: Shell and wash beans.

In glass jars: Pack raw beans into clean jars. For small-type beans, fill to 1 inch of top of jar for pints and 1½ inches for quarts; for large beans, fill to ¾ inch of top for pints and 1¼ inches for quarts. Beans should not be pressed or shaken down. Add ½ teaspoon salt to pints; 1 teaspoon to quarts. Fill jar to ½ inch of top with boiling water. Adjust jar lids. Process in pressure canner at 10 pounds pressure (240° F.).

Pint jars   40 minutes
Quart jars   50 minutes

As soon as you remove jars from canner, complete seals if necessary.

In tin cans: Pack raw beans to ¾ inch of top; do not shake or press beans down. Add ½ teaspoon salt to No. 2 cans; 1 teaspoon to No. 2½ cans. Fill cans to top with boiling water. Exhaust to 170° F. (about 10 minutes) and seal cans. Process in pressure canner at 10 pounds pressure (240° F.).

No. 2 cans   40 minutes
No. 2½ cans   40 minutes

Hot Pack: Shell the beans, cover with boiling water, and bring to boil.

In glass jars: Pack hot beans loosely to 1 inch of top. Add ½ teaspoon salt to pints; 1 teaspoon to quarts. Cover with boiling water, leaving 1-inch space at top of jar. Adjust jar lids. Process in pressure canner at 10 pounds pressure (240° F.).

Pint jars   40 minutes
Quart jars   50 minutes

As soon as you remove jars from canner, complete seals if necessary.

In tin cans: Pack hot beans loosely to ½ inch of top. Add ½ teaspoon salt to No. 2 cans; 1 teaspoon to No. 2½ cans. Fill to top with boiling water. Exhaust to 170° F. (about 10 minutes) and seal cans. Process in pressure canner at 10 pounds pressure (240° F.).

No. 2 cans   40 minutes
No. 2½ cans   40 minutes

Beans, Snap

Raw Pack: Wash beans. Trim ends; cut into 1-inch pieces.

In glass jars: Pack raw beans tightly to ½ inch of top. Add ½ teaspoon salt to pints; 1 teaspoon to quarts. Cover with boiling water, leaving ½-inch space at top of jar. Adjust jar lids. Process in pressure canner at 10 pounds pressure (240° F.).

Pint jars   20 minutes
Quart jars   25 minutes

As soon as you remove jars from canner, complete seals if necessary.

To hot pack snap beans, cover cut beans with boiling water and boil 5 minutes.

Then pack hot beans loosely in jar and cover with hot cooking liquid before processing in a pressure canner.

In tin cans: Pack raw beans tightly to ¼ inch of top. Add ½ teaspoon salt to No. 2 cans; 1 teaspoon to No. 2½ cans. Fill to top with boiling water. Exhaust to 170° F. (about 10 minutes) and seal cans. Process in pressure canner at 10 pounds pressure (240° F.).

No. 2 cans   25 minutes
No. 2½ cans   30 minutes

Hot Pack: Wash beans. Trim ends; cut into 1-inch pieces. Cover with boiling water; boil 5 minutes.

In glass jars: Pack hot beans loosely to ½ inch of top. Add ½ teaspoon salt to pints; 1 teaspoon to quarts. Cover with boiling-hot cooking liquid, leaving ½-inch space at top of jar. Adjust jar lids. Process in pressure canner at 10 pounds pressure (240° F.).

Pint jars   20 minutes
Quart jars   25 minutes

As soon as you remove jars from canner, complete seals if necessary.

In tin cans: Pack hot beans loosely to ¼ inch of top. Add ½ teaspoon salt to No. 2 cans; 1 teaspoon to No. 2½ cans. Fill to top with boiling-hot cooking liquid. Exhaust to 170° F. (about 10 minutes) and seal cans. Process in pressure canner at 10 pounds pressure (240° F.).

No. 2 cans   25 minutes
No. 2½ cans   30 minutes

Beets

Sort beets for size. Cut off tops, leaving an inch of stem. Also leave root. Wash beets. Cover with boiling water and boil until skins slip easily —15 to 25 minutes, depending on size. Skin and trim. Leave baby beets whole. Cut medium or large beets in ½-inch cubes or slices; halve or quarter very large slices.

In glass jars: Pack hot beets to ½ inch of top. Add ½ teaspoon salt to pints; 1 teaspoon to quarts. Cover with boiling water, leaving ½-inch space at top of jar. Adjust jar lids. Process in pressure canner at 10 pounds pressure (240° F.).

Pint jars   30 minutes
Quart jars   35 minutes

As soon as you remove jars from canner, complete seals if necessary.

In tin cans: Pack hot beets to ¼ inch of top. Add ½ teaspoon salt to No. 2 cans; 1 teaspoon to No. 2½ cans. Fill to top with boiling water. Exhaust to 170° F. (about 10 minutes) and seal cans. Process in pressure canner at 10 pounds pressure (240° F.).

No. 2 cans   30 minutes
No. 2½ cans   30 minutes

Beets, Pickled

See fruits.

Carrots

Raw Pack: Wash and scrape carrots. Slice or dice.

In glass jars: Pack raw carrots tightly into clean jars, to 1 inch of top of jar. Add ½ teaspoon salt to pints; 1 teaspoon to quarts. Fill jar to ½ inch of top with boiling water. Adjust jar lids. Process in pressure canner at 10 pounds pressure (240° F.).

Pint jars   25 minutes
Quart jars   30 minutes

As soon as you remove jars from canner, complete seals if necessary.

In tin cans: Pack raw carrots tightly into cans to ½ inch of top. Add ½ teaspoon salt to No. 2 cans; 1 teaspoon to No. 2½ cans. Fill cans to top with boiling water. Exhaust to 170° F. (about 10 minutes) and seal cans. Process in pressure canner at 10 pounds pressure (240° F.).

No. 2 cans   25 minutes
No. 2½ cans   30 minutes

Hot Pack: Wash and scrape carrots. Slice or dice. Cover with boiling water and bring to boil.

In glass jars: Pack hot carrots to ½ inch of top. Add ½ teaspoon salt to pints; 1 teaspoon to quarts. Cover with boiling-hot cooking liquid, leaving ½-inch space at top of jar. Adjust jar lids. Process in pressure canner at 10 pounds pressure (240° F.).

Pint jars   25 minutes
Quart jars   30 minutes

As soon as you remove jars from canner, complete seals if necessary.

In tin cans: Pack hot carrots to ¼ inch of top. Add ½ teaspoon salt to No. 2 cans; 1 teaspoon to No. 2½ cans. Fill with boiling-hot cooking liquid. Exhaust to 170° F. (about 10 minutes) and seal cans. Process in pressure canner at 10 pounds pressure (240° F.).

No. 2 cans   20 minutes
No. 2½ cans   25 minutes

Corn, Cream-Style

Raw Pack: Husk corn and remove silk. Wash. Cut corn from cob at about center of kernel and scrape cobs.

In glass jars: Use pint jars only. Pack corn to 1½ inches of top; do not shake or press down. Add ½ teaspoon salt to each jar. Fill to ½ inch of top with boiling water. Adjust jar lids. Process in pressure canner at 10 pounds pressure (240° F.).

Pint jars   95 minutes

As soon as you remove jars from canner, complete seals if necessary.

In tin cans: Use No. 2 cans only. Pack corn to ½ inch of top; do not shake or press down. Add ½ teaspoon salt to each can. Fill cans to top with boiling water. Exhaust to 170° F. (about 25 minutes) and seal cans. Process in pressure canner at 10 pounds pressure (240° F.).

No. 2 cans   105 minutes

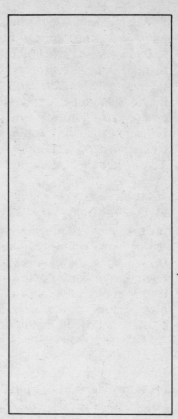

A nail driven at an angle through the cutting board (see arrow) holds the cob steady and makes it easy to cut corn from the cob.

Hot Pack: Husk corn and remove silk. Wash. Cut corn from cob at about center of kernel and scrape cob. To each quart of corn add 1 pint boiling water. Heat to boiling.

In glass jars: Use pint jars only. Pack hot corn to 1 inch of top. Add ½ teaspoon salt to each jar. Adjust jar lids. Process in pressure canner at 10 pounds pressure (240° F.).

Pint jars   85 minutes

As soon as you remove jars from canner, complete seals if necessary.

In tin cans: Use No. 2 cans only. Pack hot corn to top. Add ½ teaspoon salt to each can. Exhaust to 170° F. (about 10 minutes) and seal cans. Process in pressure canner at 10 pounds pressure (240° F.).

No. 2 cans   105 minutes

Corn, Whole-Kernel

Raw Pack: Husk corn and remove silk. Wash. Cut from cob at about two-thirds the depth of kernel.

In glass jars: Pack corn to 1 inch to top; do not shake or press down. Add ½ teaspoon salt to pints; 1 teaspoon to quarts. Fill to ½ inch of top with boiling water. Adjust jar lids. Process in pressure canner at 10 pounds pressure (240° F.).

Pint jars   55 minutes
Quart jars   85 minutes

As soon as you remove jars from canner, complete seals if necessary.

In tin cans: Pack corn to ½ inch of top; do not shake or press down. Add ½ teaspoon salt to No. 2 cans; 1 teaspoon to No. 2½ cans. Fill to top with boiling water. Exhaust to 170° F. (about 10 minutes) and seal cans. Process in pressure canner at 10 pounds pressure (240° F.).

No. 2 cans   60 minutes
No. 2½ cans   60 minutes

Hot Pack: Husk corn and remove silk. Wash. Cut from cob at about two-thirds the depth of kernel. To each quart of corn add 1 pint of boiling water. Heat to boiling.

72

In glass jars: Pack hot corn to 1 inch of top and cover with boiling-hot cooking liquid, leaving 1-inch space at top of jar. Or fill to 1 inch of top with mixture of corn and liquid. Add ½ teaspoon salt to pints; 1 teaspoon to quarts. Adjust jar lids. Process in pressure canner at 10 pounds pressure (240° F.).

Pint jars   55 minutes
Quart jars   85 minutes

As soon as you remove jars from canner, complete seals if necessary.

In tin cans: Pack hot corn to ½ inch of top and fill to top with boiling-hot cooking liquid. Or fill to top with mixture of corn and liquid. Add ½ teaspoon salt to No. 2 cans; 1 teaspoon to No. 2½ cans. Exhaust to 170° F. (about 10 minutes) and seal cans. Process in pressure canner at 10 pounds pressure (240° F.).

No. 2 cans   60 minutes
No. 2½ cans   60 minutes

To hot pack corn, put heated corn loosely in C-enamel cans; fill cans with boiling liquid.

Okra

Can only tender pods. Wash; trim. Cook for 1 minute in boiling water. Cut into 1-inch lengths or leave pods whole.

In glass jars: Pack hot okra to ½ inch of top. Add ½ teaspoon salt to pints; 1 teaspoon to quarts. Cover with boiling water, leaving ½-inch space at top of jar. Adjust jar lids. Process in pressure canner at 10 pounds pressure (240° F.).

Pint jars   25 minutes
Quart jars   40 minutes

As soon as you remove jars from canner, complete seals if necessary.

In tin cans: Pack hot okra to ¼ inch of top. Add ½ teaspoon salt to No. 2 cans; 1 teaspoon to No. 2½ cans. Fill to top with boiling water.

Exhaust to 170° F. (about 10 minutes) and seal cans. Process in pressure canner at 10 pounds pressure (240° F.).

No. 2 cans   25 minutes
No. 2½ cans   25 minutes

Peas, Fresh Blackeye (Cowpeas, Blackeye Beans)

Raw pack: Shell and wash blackeye peas.

In glass jars: Pack raw blackeye peas to 1½ inches of top of pint jars and 2 inches of top of quart jars; do not shake or press peas down. Add ½ teaspoon salt to pints; 1 teaspoon to quarts. Cover with boiling water, leaving ½-inch space at top of jars. Adjust jar lids. Process in pressure canner at 10 pounds pressure (240° F.).

Pint jars   35 minutes
Quart jars   40 minutes

As soon as you remove jars from canner, complete seals if necessary.

In tin cans: Pack raw blackeye peas to ¾ inch of top; do not shake or press down. Add ½ teaspoon salt to No. 2 cans; 1 teaspoon to No. 2½ cans. Cover with boiling water, leaving ¼-inch space at top of cans. Exhaust to 170° F. (about 10 minutes) and seal cans. Process in pressure canner at 10 pounds pressure (240° F.).

No. 2 cans   35 minutes
No. 2½ cans   40 minutes

Hot Pack: Shell and wash blackeye peas, cover with boiling water, and bring to a rolling boil. Drain.

In glass jars: Pack hot blackeye peas to 1¼ inches of top of pint jars and 1½ inches of top of quart jars; do not shake or press peas down. Add ½ teaspoon salt to pints; 1 teaspoon to quarts. Cover with boiling water, leaving ½-inch space at top of jar. Adjust jar lids. Process in pressure canner at 10 pounds pressure (240° F.).

Pint jars   35 minutes
Quart jars   40 minutes

As soon as you remove jars from canner, complete seals if necessary.

In tin cans: Pack hot blackeye peas to ½ inch of top; do not shake or press peas down. Add ½ teaspoon salt to No. 2 cans; 1 teaspoon to No. 2½ cans. Cover with boiling water, leaving ¼-inch space at top of cans. Exhaust to 170° F. (about 10 minutes) and seal cans. Process in pressure canner at 10 pounds pressure (240° F.).

No. 2 cans   30 minutes
No. 2½ cans   35 minutes

Peas, Fresh Green

In glass jars: Pack peas to 1 inch of top; do not shake or press down. Add ½ teaspoon salt to pints; 1 teaspoon to quarts. Cover with boiling water, leaving 1½ inches of space at top of jar. Adjust jar lids. Process in pressure canner at 10 pounds pressure (240° F.).

Pint jars   40 minutes
Quart jars   40 minutes

As soon as you remove jars from canner, complete seals if necessary.

In tin cans: Pack peas to ¼ inch of top; do not shake or press down. Add ½ teaspoon salt to No. 2 cans; 1 teaspoon to No. 2½ cans. Fill to top with boiling water. Exhaust to 170° F. (about 10 minutes) and seal cans. Process at 10 pounds pressure (240° F.).

No. 2 cans   30 minutes
No. 2½ cans   35 minutes

Hot Pack: Shell and wash peas. Cover with boiling water. Bring to boil.

In glass jars: Pack hot peas loosely to 1 inch of top. Add ½ teaspoon salt to pints; 1 teaspoon to quarts. Cover with boiling water, leaving 1-inch space at top of jar. Adjust jar lids. Process in pressure canner at 10 pounds pressure (240° F.).

Pint jars   40 minutes
Quart jars   40 minutes

As soon as you remove jars from canner, complete seals if necessary.

In tin cans: Pack hot peas loosely to ¼ inch of top. Add ½ teaspoon salt to No. 2 cans; 1 teaspoon to No. 2½ cans. Fill to top with boiling water. Exhaust to 170° F. (about 10 minutes) and seal cans. Process at 10 pounds pressure (240° F.).

No. 2 cans   30 minutes
No. 2½ cans   35 minutes

Potatoes, Cubed

Wash, pare, and cut potatoes into ½-inch cubes. Dip cubes in brine (1 teaspoon salt to 1 quart water) to prevent darkening. Drain. Cook for 2 minutes in boiling water, drain.

In glass jars: Pack hot potatoes to ½ inch of top. Add ½ teaspoon salt to pints; 1 teaspoon to quarts. Cover with boiling water, leaving ½-inch space at top of jar. Adjust jar lids. Process in pressure canner at 10 pounds pressure (240° F.).

Pint jars   35 minutes
Quart jars   40 minutes

As soon as you remove jars from canner, complete seals if necessary.

In tin cans: Pack hot potatoes to ¼ inch of top. Add ½ teaspoon salt to No. 2 cans; 1 teaspoon to No. 2½ cans. Fill to top with boiling water. Exhaust to 170° F. (about 10 minutes) and seal cans. Process in pressure canner at 10 pounds pressure (240° F.).

No. 2 cans   35 minutes
No. 2½ cans   40 minutes

Potatoes, Whole

Use potatoes 1 to 2½ inches in diameter. Wash, pare, and cook in boiling water for 10 minutes. Drain.

In glass jars: Pack hot potatoes to ½ inch of top. Add ½ teaspoon salt to pints; 1 teaspoon to quarts. Cover with boiling water, leaving ½-inch space at top of jar. Adjust jar lids. Process in pressure canner at 10 pounds pressure (240° F.).

Pint jars   35 minutes
Quart jars   40 minutes

As soon as you remove jars from canner, complete seals if necessary.

In tin cans: Pack hot potatoes to ¼ inch of top. Add ½ teaspoon salt to No. 2 cans; 1 teaspoon to No. 2½ cans. Fill to top with boiling water. Exhaust to 170° F. (about 10 minutes) and seal cans. Process in pressure canner at 10 pounds pressure (240° F.).

No. 2 cans   35 minutes
No. 2½ cans   40 minutes

Pumpkin, Cubed

Wash pumpkin, remove seeds, and pare. Cut into 1-inch cubes. Add just enough water to cover; bring to boil.

In glass jars: Pack hot cubes to ½ inch of top. Add ½ teaspoon salt to pints; 1 teaspoon to quarts. Cover with hot cooking liquid, leaving ½-inch space at top of jar. Adjust jar lids. Process in pressure canner at 10 pounds pressure (240° F.).

Pint jars   55 minutes
Quart jars   90 minutes

As soon as you remove jars from canner, complete seals if necessary.

In tin cans: Pack hot cubes to ¼ inch of top. Add ½ teaspoon salt to No. 2 cans; 1 teaspoon to No. 2½ cans. Fill to top with boiling water. Exhaust to 170° F. (about 10 minutes) and seal cans. Process in pressure canner at 10 pounds pressure (240° F.).

No. 2 cans	50 minutes
No. 2½ cans	75 minutes

Pumpkin, Strained

Wash pumpkin, remove seeds, and pare. Cut into 1-inch cubes. Steam until tender, about 25 minutes. Put through food mill or strainer. Simmer until heated through; stir to keep from sticking to pan.

In glass jar: Pack hot to ½ inch of top. Add no liquid or salt. Adjust jar lids. Process at 10 pounds pressure (240° F.).

Pint jars	65 minutes
Quart jars	80 minutes

As soon as you remove jars from canner, complete seals if necessary.

In tin cans: Pack hot to 1/8 inch of top. Add no liquid or salt. Exhaust to 170° F. (about 10 minutes) and seal cans. Process in pressure canner at 10 pounds pressure (240° F.).

No. 2 cans	75 minutes
No. 2½ cans	90 minutes

Spinach (and Other Greens)

Can only freshly picked, tender spinach. Pick over and wash thoroughly. Cut out tough stems and midribs. Place about 2½ pounds of spinach in a cheesecloth bag and steam about 10 minutes or until well wilted.

In glass jars: Pack hot spinach loosely to ½ inch of top. Add ¼ teaspoon salt to pints; ½ teaspoon to quarts. Cover with boiling water, leaving ½-inch space at top of jar. Adjust jar lids. Process in pressure canner at 10 pounds pressure (240° F.).

Pint jars	70 minutes
Quart jars	90 minutes

As soon as you remove jars from canner, complete seals if necessary.

In tin cans: Pack hot spinach loosely to ¼ inch of top. Add ¼ teaspoon salt to No. 2 cans; ½ teaspoon to No. 2½ cans. Fill to top with boiling water. Exhaust to 170° F. (about 10 minutes) and seal cans. Process in pressure canner at 10 pounds pressure (240° F.).

No. 2 cans	65 minutes
No. 2½ cans	75 minutes

Squash, Summer

Raw Pack: Wash but do not pare squash. Trim ends. Cut squash into ½-inch slices; halve or quarter to make pieces of uniform size.

In glass jars: Pack raw squash tightly into clean jars to 1 inch of top of jar. Add ½ teaspoon salt to pints; 1 teaspoon to quarts. Fill jar to ½ inch of top with boiling water. Adjust jar lids. Process in pressure canner at 10 pounds pressure (240° F.).

Pint jars	25 minutes
Quart jars	30 minutes

As soon as you remove jars from canner, complete seals if necessary.

In tin cans: Pack raw squash tightly into cans to ½ inch of top. Add ½ teaspoon salt to No. 2 cans; 1 teaspoon to No. 2½ cans. Fill cans to top with boiling water. Exhaust to 170° F. (about 10 minutes) and seal cans. Process in pressure canner at 10 pounds pressure (240° F.).

No. 2 cans	20 minutes
No. 2½ cans	20 minutes

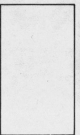

To raw pack squash, pack uniform pieces of squash tightly into jars.

Cover squash with boiling water just before closing jars and putting in pressure canner.

Hot Pack: Wash squash and trim ends; do not pare. Cut squash into ½-inch slices; halve or quarter to make pieces of uniform size. Add just enough water to cover. Bring to boil.

In glass jars: Pack hot squash loosely to ½ inch of top. Add ½ teaspoon salt to pints; 1 teaspoon to quarts. Cover with boiling-hot cooking liquid, leaving ½-inch space at top of jar. Adjust jar lids. Process in pressure canner at 10 pounds pressure (240° F.).

Pint jars   30 minutes
Quart jars   40 minutes

As soon as you remove jars from canner, complete seals if necessary.

In tin cans: Pack hot squash loosely to ¼ inch of top. Add ½ teaspoon salt to No. 2 cans; 1 teaspoon to No. 2½ cans. Fill to top with boiling-hot cooking liquid. Exhaust to 170° F. (about 10 minutes) and seal cans. Process in pressure canner at 10 pounds pressure (240° F.).

No. 2 cans   20 minutes
No. 2½ cans   20 minutes

Squash, Winter
Follow method for pumpkin.

Sweetpotatoes, Dry Pack
Wash sweetpotatoes. Sort for size. Boil or steam until partially soft (20 to 30 minutes). Skin. Cut in pieces if large.

In glass jars: Pack hot sweetpotatoes tightly to 1 inch of top, pressing gently to fill spaces. Add no salt or liquid. Adjust jar lids. Process in pressure canner at 10 pounds pressure (240° F.).

Pint jars   65 minutes
Quart jars   95 minutes

As soon as you remove jars from canner, complete seals if necessary.

In tin cans: Pack hot sweetpotatoes tightly to top of can, pressing gently to fill spaces. Add no salt or liquid. Exhaust to 170° F. (about 10 minutes) and seal cans. Process in pressure canner at 10 pounds pressure (240° F.).

No. 2 cans   80 minutes
No. 2½ cans   95 minutes

Sweetpotatoes, Wet Pack
Wash sweetpotatoes. Sort for size. Boil or steam just until skins slip easily. Skin and cut in pieces.

In glass jars: Pack hot sweetpotatoes to 1 inch of top. Add ½ teaspoon salt to pints; 1 teaspoon to quarts. Cover with boiling water or medium syrup, leaving 1-inch space at top of jar. Adjust jar lids. Process in pressure canner at 10 pounds pressure (240° F.).

Pint jars   55 minutes
Quart jars   90 minutes

As soon as you remove jars from canner, complete seals if necessary.

In tin cans: Pack hot sweetpotatoes to ¼ inch of top. Add ½ teaspoon salt to No. 2 cans; 1 teaspoon to No. 2½ cans. Fill to top with boiling water or medium syrup. Exhaust to 170° F. (about 10 minutes) and seal cans. Process in pressure canner at 10 pounds pressure (240° F.).

No. 2 cans   70 minutes
No. 2½ cans   90 minutes

Questions and Answers

Q. Is it safe to process foods in the oven?
A. No, oven canning is dangerous. Jars may explode. The temperature of the food in jars during oven processing does not get high enough to insure destruction of spoilage bacteria in vegetables.

Q. Why is open-kettle canning not recommended?
A. In open-kettle canning, food is cooked in an ordinary kettle, then packed into hot jars and sealed without processing. For vegetables, the temperatures obtained in open-kettle canning are not high enough to destroy all the spoilage organisms that may be in the food. Spoilage bacteria may get in when the food is transferred from kettle to jar.

Q. May a pressure canner be used for processing fruits and tomatoes?

A. Yes. If it is deep enough it may be used as a water-bath canner. Or you may use a pressure canner to process fruits and tomatoes at 0 to 1 pound pressure without having the containers of food completely covered with water. Put water in the canner to the shoulders of the jars; fasten cover. When live steam pours steadily from the open vent, start counting time. Leave vent open and process for the same times given for the boiling-water bath.

Q. Must glass jars and lids be sterilized by boiling before canning?
A. No, not when boiling-water bath or pressure-canner method is used. The containers as well as the food are sterilized during processing. But be sure jars and lids are clean.

Q. Why is liquid sometimes lost from glass jars during processing?
A. Loss of liquid may be due to packing jars too full, fluctuating pressure in a pressure canner, or lowering pressure too suddenly.

Q. Should liquid lost during processing be replaced?
A. No, never open a jar and refill with liquid—this would let in bacteria and you would need to process again. Loss of liquid does not cause food to spoil, though the food above the liquid may darken.

Q. Is it safe to use home canned food if liquid is cloudy?
A. Cloudy liquid may be a sign of spoilage. But it may be caused by the minerals in hard water, or by starch from overripe vegetables. If liquid is cloudy, boil the food. Do not taste or use any food that foams during heating or has an off odor.

Q. Why does canned fruit sometimes float in jars?
A. Fruit may float because pack is too loose or syrup too heavy; or because some air remains in tissues of the fruit after heating and processing.

Q. Is it safe to can foods without salt?
A. Yes. Salt is used for flavor only and is not necessary for safe processing.

Q. What makes canned foods change color?

A. Darkening of foods at the tops of jars may be caused by oxidation due to air in the jars or by too little heating or processing to destroy enzymes. Overprocessing may cause discoloration of foods throughout the containers.

Pink and blue colors sometimes seen in canned pears, apples, and peaches are caused by chemical changes in the coloring matter of the fruit.

Iron and copper from cooking utensils or from water in some localities may cause brown, black, and gray colors in some foods.

When canned corn turns brown, the discoloring may be due to the variety of corn, to stage of ripeness, to overprocessing, or to copper or iron pans.

Packing liquid may dissolve coloring materials from the foods. The use of plain tin cans will cause some foods to lose color.

Q. Is it safe to eat discolored canned foods?
A. The color changes noted above do not mean the food is unsafe to eat. However, spoilage may also cause color changes. Any canned food that has an unusual color should be examined carefully before use.

Q. Does ascorbic acid (Vitamin C) help keep fruits and vegetables from darkening?
A. Yes. The addition of ¼ teaspoon of crystalline ascorbic acid (Vitamin C) to a quart of fruit or vegetable before it is processed retards oxidation, which is one cause of darkening of canned foods. One teaspoon of crystalline ascorbic acid weighs about 3 grams (or 3,000 milligrams).

Q. Is it all right to use preservatives in home canning?
A. No. Some canning powders or other chemical preservatives may be harmful.

Q. Why do the undersides of metal lids sometimes discolor?
A. Natural compounds in some foods corrode the metal and make a brown or black deposit on the underside of the lid. This deposit is harmless.

Q. When canned or frozen fruits are bought in large containers, is it possible to can them in smaller containers?
A. Any canned or frozen fruit may be heated through, packed, and processed the same length

of time as recommended for hot packs. This canned food may be of lower quality than if fruit had been canned when fresh.

Q. Is it safe to leave food in tin cans after opening?
A. Yes. Food in tin cans needs only to be covered and refrigerated.

Q. Is the processing time the same no matter what kind of range is used?
A. Processing times and temperatures are for canning in a pressure canner or boiling-water bath with any type of range.

Q. Can fruits and vegetables be canned without heating if aspirin is used?
A. No. Aspirin cannot be relied on to prevent spoilage or to give satisfactory products. Adequate heat treatment is the only safe procedure.

Q. Where should I store canned goods?
A. The best storage for canned foods is in a dry place at moderately cool, but not freezing temperatures. Avoid storage near steam pipes, radiators, furnaces, and kitchen ranges.

Q. How long will canned foods keep?
A. This will depend upon a number of factors such as the type of food canned, the processing it has received, how it has been handled, and the conditions under which it has been stored. Generally speaking, if the can itself is normal in appearance, the food inside should still be wholesome. However, a regular turnover about once a year is suggested.

Q. What effect does freezing have on canned foods?
A. A slight breakdown of texture may occur in a few products, but otherwise a single freezing and thawing does not affect canned foods adversely. Some creamy foods may curdle or separate upon freezing but heating usually restores the original consistency.

During freezing, the contents of a can expand, put a strain on the can seams, and cause the ends to bulge. Check the container carefully after thawing, to be sure that the ends return to their normal flat appearance. If they do not, air has gotten into the can, and the contents will not keep.

Q. Does damage to the outside of the can mean the food is unsuitable for use?
A. Not necessarily. Rust or dents do not affect the contents of the can as long as the can does not leak. However, if the can is leaking, or if the ends are bulged, or if the contents have an abnormal odor or appearance, discard the can without tasting the contents. In such cases, spoilage may have taken place.

Q. Are metal fragments in canned foods harmful?
A. Investigations have shown that metal slivers which get into food cans when they are opened by can openers are not injurious to health. However, metal fragments are undesirable, and you should make every effort to keep them out of foods. Keep can openers sharp, clean, and in good working order.

Q. Can opened canned food be kept safely under refrigeration?
A. Yes. Opened canned food should be refrigerated as you would any other cooked food. However, if the opened food is to be kept for a substantial period of time, it may be tightly covered, frozen, and held frozen until use. Transfer to plastic freezer bags of appropriate size before freezing will assist in excluding oxygen and minimize drying. However, there may be some softening of texture.

FREEZING

Freezing Your Home Grown Fruits and Vegetables

There is no "out of season" for products of your garden and orchard—if you have a home freezer.

Freezing is one of the simplest and least time-consuming ways to preserve foods at home. It keeps well the natural color, fresh flavor, and nutritive values of most fruits and vegetables. Frozen fruits and vegetables are ready to serve on short notice because most of the preparation they need for the table is done before freezing.

Directions are given in this book for freezing many fruits and vegetables that give satisfactory products when frozen at home. It is important that the directions be followed carefully, because the quality of product can vary with freshness of produce used, method of preparation and packaging, and conditions of freezing.

GENERAL FREEZING PROCEDURES
Freezing is not necessarily recommended as the preferred way for preserving all products. What to freeze must be decided on the basis of family needs and desires, on freezer space and cost of freezer storage, and on other storage facilities available.

It may be more economical, for instance, to store some fruits and vegetables in a vegetable cellar than to freeze them. But to you freezing may be worth the extra cost because of the convenience of having the products prepared so they can be readied quickly for serving.

Costs of owning and operating a home freezer vary with the rate of turnover of foods, electricity used, costs of packaging materials, repairs, and the original price of the freezer.

Some varieties of all fruits and vegetables freeze better than others. Because growing conditions differ widely throughout the country and different varieties of fruits and vegetables are available in different localities, it is not practical to specify here the varieties suitable for freezing.

If you have doubt as to how well a fruit or vegetable will freeze, it would be well to test it before freezing large quantities. To test, freeze three or four packages and sample the food after freezing. This shows the effect of freezing only, not the effect of storage.

Some fruits and vegetables do not make satisfactory products when frozen. They include green onions, lettuce and other salad greens, radishes, tomatoes (except as juice or cooked).

Containers for Freezing
The prime purpose of packaging is to keep food from drying out and to preserve food value, flavor, color, and pleasing texture.

All containers should be easy to seal and waterproof so they will not leak. Packaging materials must be durable and must not become so brittle at low temperatures that they crack.

To retain highest quality in frozen food, packaging materials should be moisture-vapor-proof, to prevent evaporation. Many of the packaging materials on the market for frozen food are not moisture-vapor-proof, but are sufficiently moisture-vapor resistant to retain satisfactory quality of fruits and vegetables during storage. Glass, metal, and rigid plastic are examples of moisture-vapor-proof packaging materials. Most bags, wrapping materials, and waxed cartons made especially for freezing are moisture-vapor-resistant. Not sufficiently moisture-vapor-resistant to be suitable for packaging foods to be frozen are ordinary waxed papers, and paper cartons from cottage cheese, ice cream, and milk.

Rigid containers. Rigid containers made of aluminum, glass, plastic, tin, or heavily waxed cardboard are suitable for all packs, and especially good for liquid packs. Glass canning jars may be used for freezing most fruits and vegetables except those packed in water. Plain tin or R-enamel cans may be used for all foods, but some foods may be better packed in cans with special enamel linings: C-enamel for foods containing considerable sulfur—corn, lima beans, carrots; R-enamel for highly colored foods—beets, berries, red cherries, fruit juices, plums, pumpkin, rhubarb, squash, sweetpotatoes.

Nonrigid containers. Bags and sheets of moisture-vapor-resistant cellophane, heavy aluminum foil, pliofilm, polyethylene, or laminated papers and duplex bags consisting of various combinations of paper, metal foil, glassine, cellophane, and rubber latex are suitable for dry-packed vegetables and fruits. Bags also can be used for liquid packs.

Bags and sheets are used with or without outer cardboard cartons to protect against tearing. Bags without a protective carton are difficult to stack. The sheets may be used for wrapping such foods as corn-on-the-cob or asparagus. Some of the sheets may be heat-sealed to make a bag of the size you need. Sheets that are heat-sealed on both sides may be used as outer wraps for folding paperboard cartons.

Size. Select a size that will hold only enough of a fruit or vegetable for one meal for your family.

Shape. Rigid containers that are flat on both top and bottom stack well in a freezer. Round containers and those with flared sides or raised bottoms waste freezer space. Nonrigid containers that bulge waste freezer space.

Food can be removed easily, before it is thawed, from containers with sides that are straight from bottom to top or that flare out. Food must be partially thawed before it can be removed from containers with openings narrower than the body of the container.

Bags, sheets, and folding paperboard cartons take up little room when not in use. Rigid containers with flared sides will stack one inside the other and save space in your cupboard when not in use. Those with straight sides or narrow top openings cannot be nested.

Sealing. Care in sealing is as important as using the right container. Rigid containers usually are sealed either by pressing on or screwing on the lid. Tin cans such as are used in home canning require a sealing machine or special lids. Some rigid cardboard cartons need to have freezer tape or special wax applied after sealing to make them airtight and leakproof. Glass jars must be sealed with a lid containing composition rubber or with a lid and a rubber ring.

Most bags used for packaging can be heat-sealed or sealed by twisting and folding back the top of the bag and securing with a string, a good quality rubber or plastic band, or other sealing device available on the market. Some duplex bags are sealed by folding over a metal strip attached to the top of the bag.

Special equipment for heat-sealing bags or sheets for freezing is available on the market, or a household iron may be used. To heat-seal polyethylene or pliofilm bags or sheets used as overwraps, first place a piece of paper or heat-resistant material made especially for the purpose over the edges to be sealed. Then press with a warm iron. Regulate heat of the iron carefully—too much heat melts or crinkles the materials and prevents sealing.

Reuse. Tin cans (with slip-top closures), glass, rigid plastic, and aluminum containers can be reused indefinitely. It is difficult to reuse aluminum foil boxes, because edges of lids and containers are folded over in sealing. Tin cans that require a sealer must be reflanged with a special attachment to a sealer before they are reused. A tin can or lid that is dented should not be used if it cannot be sealed.

Reuse of rigid cardboard cartons, unless plastic-lined, is not generally advisable because cleaning is difficult. Folding paperboard cartons used to protect an inner bag can be reused.

Cost. When you compare prices of the containers that are available in your locality, consider whether they will be reusable or not. If containers are reusable, a higher initial cost may be a saving in the long run.

Care of Packaging Materials. Protect packaging materials from dust and insects. Keep bags and rolls of wrapping materials that may become brittle, such as cellophane, in a place that is cool and not too dry.

Freezing accessories. Check on other items that help make packaging easier. Some containers are easier to fill if you use a stand and funnel. Special sealing irons available on the market or a regular household iron may be used for heat-sealing bags, wrappers, and some type of paper cartons. With some sealing irons, a small wooden block or box makes sealing of bags easier and quicker.

Packing

Pack food and syrup cold into containers. Having materials cold speeds up freezing and helps retain natural color, flavor, and texture of food.

Pack foods tightly to cut down on the amount of air in the package.

When food is packed in bags, press air out of unfilled part of bag. Press firmly to prevent air from getting back in. Seal immediately, allowing the head space recommended for the product.

Allow ample head space. With only a few exceptions, allowance for head space is needed between packed food and closure because food expands as it freezes. A guide to the amount of head space to allow follows.

Liquid pack (fruit packed in juice, sugar, syrup, or water; crushed or puree; juice): for tall, either straight or slightly flared containers with wide top openings allow ½ inch for a pint and 1 inch for a quart container. For the same shape container with a narrow top opening allow ¾ inch in pint and 1½ inch in quart containers.

Always allow 1½ inches head space for juice, either in pint or quart containers.

Dry pack (fruit or vegetable packed without added sugar or liquid): for tall, either straight or slightly flared containers with wide or narrow top openings allow ½ inch in both pint and quart-size containers. Vegetables that pack loosely, such as broccoli and asparagus, require no head space.

Keep sealing edges free from moisture or food so that a good closure can be made. Seal carefully.

Label packages plainly. Include name of food, date it was packed, and type of pack if food is packed in more than one form. Gummed labels, colored tape, crayons, pens, and stamps are made especially for labeling frozen food packages.

Loading the Freezer

Freeze fruits and vegetables soon after they are packed. Put them in the freezer a few packages at a time as you have them ready, or keep packages in the refrigerator until all you are doing at one time are ready. Then transfer them to the home freezer. Freeze at 0° F. or below.

Put no more unfrozen food into a home freezer than will freeze within 24 hours. Usually this will be about 2 or 3 pounds of food to each cubic foot of its capacity. Overloading slows down the rate of freezing, and foods that freeze too slowly may lose quality or spoil. For quickest freezing, place packages against freezing plates or coils and leave a little space between packages so air can circulate freely.

After freezing, packages may be stored close together. Store them at 0° F. or below. At higher temperatures foods lose quality much faster. Most fruits and vegetables maintain high quality for 8 to 12 months at 0° or below; citrus fruits and citrus juices, for 4 to 6 months. Unsweetened fruits lose quality faster than those packed in sugar or syrup. Longer storage will not make foods unfit for use, but may impair quality.

It's a good idea to post a list of frozen foods near the freezer and keep it up to date. List foods as you put them in freezer, with date; check foods off the list as you remove them.

Refreezing

Occasionally, frozen foods are partially or completely thawed before it is discovered that the freezer is not operating.

The basis for safety in refreezing foods is the temperature at which thawed foods have been held and the length of time they were held after thawing.

You may safely refreeze frozen foods that have thawed if they still contain ice crystals or if they are still cold—about 40° F.—and have been held no longer than 1 or 2 days at refrigerator temperature after thawing. In general, if a food is safe to eat, it is safe to refreeze.

Even partial thawing and refreezing reduce quality of fruits and vegetables. Foods that have been frozen and thawed require the same care as foods that have never been frozen. Use refrozen foods as soon as possible to save as much of their quality as you can.

POINTS ON FREEZING FRUITS

Most fruits can be frozen satisfactorily, but the quality of the frozen product will vary with the kind of fruit, stage of maturity, and type of pack. Pointers on selecting fruit properly are given in the directions and must be followed carefully to be sure of a good frozen product.

Generally, flavor is well retained by freezing. Texture may be somewhat softer than that of fresh fruit. Some fruits require special treatment when packed to make them more pleasing in color, texture, or flavor after thawing. Most fruits are best frozen soon after harvesting. Some, such as peaches and pears, may need to be held a short time to ripen.

Before Packing

All fruits need to be washed in cold water. Wash a small quantity at a time to save undue handling, which may bruise delicate fruits such as berries. A perforated or wire basket is useful. Lift washed fruits out of the water and drain thoroughly. Don't let the fruit stand in the water—some lose food value and flavor that way and some get watersoaked.

In general, fruit is prepared for freezing in about the same way as for serving. Large fruits generally make a better product if cut in pieces or crushed before freezing. Many fruits can be frozen successfully in several forms. Good parts of less perfect fruit are suitable for crushed or pureed packs.

Peel, trim, pit and slice fruit following the directions that follow. It is best to prepare enough fruit for only a few containers at one time, especially those fruits that darken rapidly. Two or three quarts is a good quantity to work with.

If directions call for fruit to be crushed, suit the method of crushing to the fruit. For soft fruits, a wire potato masher, pastry fork, or slotted spoon may be used; if fruits are firm they may be crushed more easily with a food chopper. For making purees a colander, food press, or strainer is useful.

Use equipment of aluminum, earthenware, enameled ware, glass, nickel, stainless steel, or good-quality tinware. Do not use galvanized ware in direct contact with fruit or fruit juices because the acid in fruit dissolves zinc, which is poisonous.

Metallic off-flavors may result from the use of iron utensils, chipped enameled ware, or tinware that is not well tinned.

Ways to Pack

Most fruits have better texture and flavor if packed in sugar or syrup. Some may be packed without sweetening.

In the directions for freezing, three ways of packing are given for fruits whole or in pieces—syrup pack, sugar pack, and unsweetened pack. Directions are also given for packing crushed fruits, purees, and fruit juices.

Your selection of the way to pack the fruit will depend on the intended use. Fruits packed in a syrup are generally best for dessert use; those packed in dry sugar or unsweetened are best for most cooking purposes because there is less liquid in the product.

Syrup Pack. A 40-percent syrup is recommended for most fruits. For some mild-flavored fruits lighter syrups are desirable to prevent masking of flavor. Heavier syrups may be needed for very sour fruits.

In the directions for each fruit, syrups are called for according to the percentage of sugar in the syrup. Below is a master recipe from which any of the syrups can be made. It takes one-half to two-thirds cup of syrup for each pint package of fruit.

Syrups for Use in Freezing Fruits

Type	Sugar Cups	Water Cups	Yield Cups
30-percent	2	4	5
35-percent	2½	4	5⅓
40-percent	3	4	5½
50-percent	4¾	4	6½
60-percent	7	4	7¾
65-percent	8¾	4	8⅔

Dissolve sugar in cold or hot water. If hot water is used, cool syrup before using. Syrup may be made up the day before and kept cold in the refrigerator.

When packing fruit into containers be sure the syrup covers the fruit so that the top pieces will not change in color and flavor. To keep the fruit under the syrup, place a small piece of crumpled parchment paper or other water-resistant wrapping material on top and press fruit down into syrup before closing and sealing the container.

Sugar Pack. Cut fruit into a bowl or shallow pan. Sprinkle the sugar (quantity needed given in the directions for each fruit) over the fruit. To mix, use a large spoon or pancake turner. Mix gently until juice is drawn out and sugar is dissolved.

Put fruit and juice into containers. Place a small piece of crumpled parchment paper or other water-resistant wrapping material on top to hold fruit down in juice. Close and seal the container.

Unsweetened Pack. Pack prepared fruit into containers, without added liquid or sweetening, or cover with water containing ascorbic acid (Vitamin C). Or pack crushed or sliced fruit in its own juice without sweetening. Press fruit down into juice or water with a small piece of crumpled parchment paper as for syrup and sugar pack. Close and seal containers.

To Keep Fruit from Darkening

Some fruits darken during freezing if not treated to retard darkening. Directions for such fruits list antidarkening treatment as part of the freezing preparation. Several types of antidarkening treatments are used because all fruits are not protected equally well by all treatments.

Ascorbic acid (Vitamin C). For most of the fruits that need antidarkening treatment, ascorbic acid (Vitamin C) may be used. This is very effective in preserving color and flavor of fruit and adds nutritive value.

Ascorbic acid in crystalline form is available at drug stores in various sized containers from 25 to 1,000 grams. (Crystalline ascorbic acid may be obtained also in powdered form.) One teaspoon weighs about 3 grams; thus there are approximately 8 teaspoons of ascorbic acid in a 25-gram container. In the recipes, amounts of crystalline ascorbic acid are given in teaspoons.

In syrup pack. Add the dissolved ascorbic acid to the cold syrup shortly before using. Stir in gently so you won't stir in air. Solutions of ascorbic acid should be made up as needed. Keep syrup in refrigerator until used.

In sugar pack. Sprinkle the dissolved ascorbic acid over the fruit just before adding water.

In unsweetened pack. Sprinkle the dissolved ascorbic acid over the fruit and mix thoroughly just before packing. If fruit is packed in water, dissolve the ascorbic acid in the water.

In fruit juices. Add ascorbic acid directly to the juice. Stir only enough to dissolve ascorbic acid.

In crushed fruits and fruit purees. Add dissolved ascorbic acid to the fruit preparation and mix.

Citric acid, lemon juice. For a few fruits citric acid or lemon juice (which contains both citric acid and ascorbic acid) makes a suitable antidarkening agent. However, neither is as effective as ascorbic acid. Citric acid or lemon juice in the large quantities needed in some cases would mask the natural fruit flavors or make the fruits too sour.

Citric acid in crystalline or powdered form is available at drugstores. When using citric acid, dissolve it in a little cold water before adding to the fruit according to directions for that fruit.

Steam. For some fruits steaming for a few minutes before packing is enough to control darkening.

Table of Fruit Yields

The following table will help you figure how much frozen fruit you can get from a given

FRUIT	FRESH, AS PURCHASED OR PICKED	FROZEN
Apples	1 bu. (48 lb.)	32 to 40 pt.
	1 box (44 lb.)	29 to 35 pt.
	1 ¼ to 1 ½ lb.	1 pt.
Cantaloups	1 dozen (28 lb.)	22 pt.
	1 to 1 ¼ lb.	1 pt.
Cherries, sweet or sour	1 bu. (56 lb.)	36 to 44 pt.
	1 ¼ to 1 ½ lb.	1 pt.
Currants	2 qt. (3 lb.)	4 pt.
	¾ lb.	1 pt.
Peaches	1 bu. (48 lb.)	32 to 48 pt.
	1 lug box (20 lb.)	13 to 20 pt.
	1 to 1 ½ lb.	1 pt.
Pears	1 bu. (50 lb.)	40 to 50 pt.
	1 western box (46 lb.)	37 to 46 pt.
	1 to 1 ¼ lb.	1 pt.
Plums and prunes	1 bu. (56 lb.)	38 to 56 pt.
	1 crate (20 lb.)	13 to 20 pt.
	1 to 1 ½ lb.	1 pt.
Rhubarb	15 lb.	15 to 22 pt.
	⅔ to 1 lb.	1 pt.
Strawberries	1 crate (24 qt.)	38 pt.
	⅔ qt.	1 pt.

quantity of fresh fruit and will help in making cost comparisons.

The number of pints of frozen food you can get depends upon the quality, variety, maturity and size of the fruit—and whether it is frozen whole or in halves, in slices, in cubes, or in balls.

DIRECTIONS FOR FRUITS

Apples, slices

Syrup pack is preferred for apples to be used for fruit cocktail or uncooked dessert. Apples packed in sugar or frozen unsweetened are good for pie making. For better quality, apple slices need to be treated to prevent darkening.

Select full-flavored apples that are crisp and firm, not mealy in texture. Wash, peel, and core. Slice medium apples into twelfths, large ones into sixteenths.

Pack in one of the following ways:

Syrup pack. Use 40-percent syrup. For a better quality frozen product add 1/2 teaspoon crystalline ascorbic acid to each quart of syrup.

Slice apples directly into cold syrup in container, starting with 1/2 cup syrup to a pint container. Press fruit down in containers and add enough syrup to cover. Leave head space. Seal and freeze.

Sugar pack. To prevent darkening of apples during preparation, slice them into a solution of 2 tablespoons salt to a gallon of water. Hold in this solution no more than 15 to 20 minutes. Drain.

To retard darkening, place slices in a single layer in steamer; steam 1-1/2 to 2 minutes, depending on thickness of slice. Cool in cold water; drain.

Over each quart (1-1/4 pounds) of apple slices sprinkle evenly 1/2 cup sugar and stir.

Pack apples into containers and press fruit down, leaving head space. Seal and freeze.

Unsweetened pack. Follow directions for sugar pack, omitting sugar.

Applesauce

Select full-flavored apples. Wash apples, peel if desired, core, and slice. To each quart of apple slices add 1/3 cup water; cook until tender. Cool and strain if necessary. Sweeten to taste with 1/4 to 3/4 cup sugar for each quart (2 pounds) of sauce.

Pack into containers, leaving head space. Seal and freeze.

Cherries, Sour

Whole. Syrup pack is best for cherries to be served uncooked. Sugar pack is preferable for cherries to be used for pies or other cooked products. Select bright-red, tree-ripened cherries. Stem, sort, and wash thoroughly. Drain and pit. Use one of the following packs:

Syrup pack. Pack cherries into containers and cover with cold 60- or 65-percent syrup, depending on tartness of the cherries. Leave head space. Seal and freeze.

Sugar pack. To 1 quart (1-1/3 pounds) cherries add 3/4 cup sugar. Mix until sugar is dissolved. Pack into containers, leaving head space. Seal and freeze.

Crushed. Prepare for packing as for whole sour cherries. Crush coarsely. To 1 quart (2 pounds) fruit add 1 to 1-1/2 cups sugar, depending on sweetness desired. Mix thoroughly until sugar is dissolved. Pack into containers, leaving head space. Seal and freeze.

Puree. Select and prepare for packing same as for whole cherries. Then crush cherries, heat to boiling point, cool, and press through a sieve. To 1 quart (2 pounds) fruit puree add 3/4 cup sugar. Pack puree into containers, leaving head space. Seal and freeze.

Juice. Select and prepare as for whole sour cherries. Then crush cherries, heat slightly to start flow of juice, and strain juice through a jelly bag. Cool, let stand overnight, and pour off clear juice for freezing. Or juice may be packed as soon as it cools, then strained when it is thawed for serving. Sweeten with 1-1/2 to 2 cups sugar to each quart of juice or pack without

added sugar. Pour into containers, leaving head space. Seal and freeze.

Cherries, Sweet

Whole. Sweet cherries should be prepared quickly to avoid color and flavor changes. Red varieties are best for freezing. Select well-colored, tree-ripened fruit with a sweet flavor. Sort, stem, wash, and drain. Remove pits if desired; they tend to give an almond-like flavor to the fruit. Pack cherries into containers. Cover with cold 40-percent syrup, to which has been added 1/2 teaspoon crystalline ascorbic acid to the quart. Leave head space. Seal and freeze.

With sour cherries. Use half sweet cherries, half sour. Pack as above using 50-percent syrup. Ascorbic acid may be added, but is not essential as it is for sweet cherries alone.

Crushed. Prepare cherries as for freezing whole. Remove pits and crush cherries coarsely. To each quart (2 pounds) of crushed fruit add 1-1/2 cups sugar and 1/4 teaspoon crystalline ascorbic acid. Mix well. Pack into containers, leaving head space. Seal and freeze.

Juice. Frozen sweet cherry juice may lack flavor and tartness. For a tastier product, add some sour cherry juice—either before freezing or after thawing. Select well-colored, tree-ripened fruit. Sort, stem, wash, and drain. Remove pits and crush.

For red cherries, heat slightly (to 165° F.) to start flow of juice. Do not boil. Extract juice in a jelly bag.

For white cherries, extract juice without heating. Then warm juice (to 165° F.) in a double boiler or over low heat.

For either red or white cherry juice, cool the juice, let stand overnight, and pour off clear juice for freezing. Or pack the juice as soon as it cools; then strain after thawing for serving. Sweeten with 1 cup sugar to each quart of juice, or pack without adding sugar. Pour into container, leaving head space. Seal and freeze.

Currants

Whole. Select plump, fully ripe bright-red currants. Wash in cold water and remove stems. Pack in any of the following ways:

Unsweetened pack. Pack into containers, leaving head space. Seal and freeze.

Syrup pack. Pack into containers and cover currants with cold 50-percent syrup, leaving head space. Seal and freeze.

Sugar pack. To each quart (1-1/3 pounds) of fruit add 3/4 cup sugar. Stir until most of the sugar is dissolved. Pack currants into containers, leaving head space. Seal and freeze.

Crushed. Prepare as directed for whole currants. Crush. To 1 quart (2 pounds) crushed currants add 1-1/8 cups sugar. Mix until sugar is dissolved. Pack into containers, leaving head space. Seal and freeze.

Juice. For use in beverages, select as directed for whole currants. For use in jelly making, mix slightly underripe and ripe fruit. Wash in cold water and remove stems. Crush currants and warm (to 165° F.) over low heat to start flow of juice. Do not boil. Press hot fruit in jelly bag to extract juice. Cool. Sweeten with 3/4 to 1 cup sugar to each quart of juice, or pack without adding sugar. Pour into containers, leaving head space. Seal and freeze.

Fruit Cocktail

Use any combination of fruits desired . . . sliced or cubed peaches or apricots, melon balls, orange or grapefruit sections, whole seedless grapes, Bing cherries, or pineapple wedges.

Pack into containers; cover with cold 30-or 40-percent syrup, depending on fruits used. leave head space. Seal and freeze.

Peaches . . . Packed in Syrup

Peaches packed in either syrup or sugar make an excellent frozen product. Sliced peaches are shown being packed in syrup. A pint glass freezer jar is used here, but other sizes and types of containers are suitable.

Follow these general directions for packing other fruits in syrup. Vary the syrup as called for in the directions for each fruit.

Make up syrup ahead of time so it will be ready and cold when you need it. Peaches are best packed in a 40-percent syrup—3 cups of sugar to 4 cups of water. This amount makes about 5-1/2 cups of syrup. You need about 2/3 cup of syrup for each pint container of peaches.

For frozen peaches with better color and flavor, add ascorbic acid to the cold syrup as described. For peaches, use 1/2 teaspoon crystalline ascorbic acid to each quart of syrup.

Select mature peaches that are firm-ripe, with no green color in the skins. Allow 1 to

1-1/2 pounds fresh peaches for each pint to be frozen. Wash them carefully and drain.

Pit peaches, and peel them by hand for the best-looking product. Peaches peel more quickly if they are dipped first in boiling water, then cold—but have ragged edges after thawing.

Pour about 1/2 cup cold syrup into each pint container. Slice peaches directly into container.

Add syrup to cover peaches. Leave 1/2-inch head space at top of wide-mouth pint containers such as these, to allow for the expansion of the fruit during freezing.

Put a small piece of crumpled parchment paper on top of fruit to keep peaches down in the syrup. Syrup should always cover fruit to keep top pieces from changing color and flavor.

Wipe all sealing edges clean for a good seal. Screw lid on tight. Label with name of fruit and date of freezing.

Put sealed containers in the coldest part of freezer or locker. Leave a little space between containers so air can circulate freely. After fruit is frozen, store at 0° F. or below.

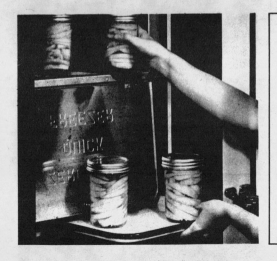

Halves and slices. Peaches in halves and slices have better quality when packed in syrup or with sugar, but a water pack will serve if sweetening is not desired.

Sugar pack. To each quart (1-1/3 pounds) of prepared fruit add 2/3 cup sugar and mix well. To retard darkening, sprinkle ascorbic acid dissolved in water over the peaches before adding sugar. Use 1/4 teaspoon crystalline ascorbic acid in 1/4 cup cold water to each quart of fruit. Pack into containers, leaving head space. Seal and freeze.

Water pack. Pack peaches into containers and cover with cold water containing 1 teaspoon crystalline ascorbic acid to each quart of water. Leave head space. Seal and freeze.

Crushed or puree. To loosen skins, dip peaches in boiling water 1/2 to 1 minute. The riper the fruit the less scalding needed. Cool in cold water, remove skins, and pit.

Crush peaches coarsely. Or, for puree, press through a sieve, or heat pitted peaches 4 minutes in just enough water to prevent scorching and then press through a sieve. With each quart (2 pounds) of crushed or pureed peaches mix 1 cup sugar. For better quality, add 1/8 teaspoon crystalline ascorbic acid to each quart of fruit. Pack into containers, leaving head space. Seal and freeze.

Pears
Halves or quarters. Select pears that are well ripened and firm but not hard. Wash fruit in cold water. Peel, cut in halves or quarters, and remove cores. Heat pears in boiling 40-percent syrup for 1 to 2 minutes, depending on size of pieces. Drain and cool. Pack pears into containers and cover with cold 40-percent syrup. For a better product, add 3/4 teaspoon crystalline ascorbic acid to a quart of cold syrup. Leave head space. Seal and freeze.

Puree. Select well-ripened pears, firm but not hard or gritty. Peel or not as desired, but do not dip in boiling water to remove skins. Prepare and pack as for peach puree.

Plums and Prunes
Whole, halves, or quarters. Frozen plums and prunes are very good for use in pies and jams, or in salads and desserts. The unsweetened pack is preferred for plums to be used for jams. Choose firm tree-ripened fruit of deep color. Sort and wash. Leave whole or cut in halves or quarters.

Pack in one of the following ways:

Unsweetened pack. Pack whole fruit into containers, leaving head space. Seal and freeze. To serve uncooked, dip frozen fruit in cold water for 5 to 10 seconds, remove skins, and cover with 40-percent syrup to thaw.

Syrup pack. Pack cut fruit into containers. Cover fruit with cold 40- or 50-percent syrup depending on tartness of fruit. For improved quality, add 1/2 teaspoon crystalline ascorbic acid to a quart of syrup. Leave head space. Seal and freeze.

Puree. Select fully ripe fruit. Wash, cut in halves, and remove pits. Puree may be prepared from unheated or heated fruit, depending on softness of fruit. To prepare puree from unheated fruit, press raw fruit through a sieve. For better quality, add either 1/4 teaspoon crystalline ascorbic acid or 1/2 tablespoon crystalline citric acid to each quart (2 pounds) of puree.

To prepare puree from heated fruit, add 1 cup water for each 4 quarts (4 pounds) of fruit. Bring to a boil, cook 2 minutes, cool, and press through a sieve.

With each quart (2 pounds) of puree, mix 1/2 to 1 cup sugar, depending on tartness of fruit. Pack into containers, leaving head space. Seal and freeze.

Juice. For juice to be served in beverages, select plums as for puree. For juice to be used for jelly making, select as recommended in specific jelly recipe. Wash plums, then simmer until soft in enough water to barely cover. Strain through a jelly bag. Cool. If desired, sweeten with 1 to 2 cups sugar for each quart of juice, depending on tartness of fruit. Pour into containers, leaving head space. Seal and freeze.

Rhubarb

Stalks or pieces. Choose firm, tender, well-colored stalks with good flavor and few fibers. Wash, trim, and cut into 1- or 2-inch pieces or in lengths to fit the package. Heating rhubarb in boiling water for 1 minute and cooling promptly in cold water helps retain color and flavor.

Unsweetened pack. Pack either raw or preheated rhubarb tightly into containers without sugar. Leave head space. Seal and freeze.

Syrup pack. Pack either raw or preheated rhubarb tightly into containers, cover with cold 40-percent syrup. Leave head space. Seal and freeze.

Puree. Prepare rhubarb as for rhubarb stalks or pieces. Add 1 cup water to 1-1/2 quarts (2 pounds) rhubarb and boil 2 minutes. Cool and press through a sieve. With 1 quart (2 pounds) puree mix 2/3 cup sugar. Pack into containers, leaving head space. Seal and freeze.

Juice. Select as for rhubarb stalks or pieces. Wash, trim, and cut into pieces 4 to 6 inches long. Add 1 quart water to 4 quarts (5 pounds) rhubarb and bring just to a boil. Press hot fruit in jelly bag to extract juice. Cool. Sweeten, if desired, using 1/2 cup sugar to a quart of juice. Pour into containers, leaving head space. Seal and freeze.

Strawberries . . . Packed in Sugar

Pride of the freezer are strawberries—sliced, sweetened with dry sugar, and frozen. For other fruits packed in sugar, follow the general steps shown here.

Whole. Choose firm, ripe, red berries preferable with a slightly tart flavor. Large berries are better sliced or crushed. Sort berries, wash them in cold water, drain well, and remove hulls. Sugar and syrup packs make better quality frozen strawberries than berries packed without sweetening.

Syrup pack. Put berries into containers and cover with cold 50-percent syrup, leaving head space. Seal and freeze.

Sugar pack. Add 3/4 cup sugar to 1 quart (1-1/3 pounds) strawberries and mix thoroughly. Put into containers, leaving head space. Seal and freeze.

Unsweetened pack. Pack into containers, leaving head space. For better color, cover with water containing 1 teaspoon crystalline ascorbic acid to each quart of water. Seal and freeze.

Sliced or crushed. Prepare for packing as for whole strawberries; then slice, or crush partially or completely. To 1 quart (1-1/2 pounds) berries add 3/4 cup sugar; mix thoroughly. Pack into containers, leaving head space. Seal and freeze.

Puree. Prepare strawberries as for freezing whole. Then press berries through a sieve. To 1 quart (2 pounds) puree add 2/3 cup sugar and mix well. Put into containers, leaving head space. Seal and freeze.

Juice. Choose fully ripe berries. Sort and wash them in cold water. Drain well and remove hulls. Crush berries and strain juice through a jelly bag. Sweeten with 2/3 to 1 cup sugar to each quart of juice, or leave unsweetened. Pour into containers, leaving head space. Seal and freeze.

POINTS ON FREEZING VEGETABLES

Best for freezing are fresh, tender vegetables right from the garden. The fresher the vegetable when frozen, the more satisfactory will be your product.

First Steps

Washing is the first step in the preparation of most vegetables for freezing. However, lima beans, green peas, and other vegetables that are protected by pods may not need to be washed.

Wash vegetables thoroughly in cold water. Lift them out of the water as grit settles to the bottom of the pan.

Sort vegetables according to size for heating and packing unless they are to be cut into pieces of uniform size.

Peel, trim, and cut into pieces, as directed for each vegetable.

Heating Before Packing

An important step in preparing vegetables for freezing is heating or "blanching" before packing. Practically every vegetable, except green pepper, maintains better quality in frozen storage if heated before packing.

The reason for heating vegetables before freezing is that it slows or stops the action of anzymes. Up until the time vegetables are ready to pick, enzymes help them grow and mature. After that they cause loss of flavor and color. If vegetables are not heated enough the enzymes continue to be active during frozen storage. Then the vegetables may develop off-flavors, discolor, or toughen so that they may be unappetizing in a few weeks. Heating also wilts or softens vegetables and makes them easier to pack. Heating time varies with the vegetable and size of pieces.

To heat in boiling water. For home freezing, the most satisfactory way to heat practically all vegetables is in boiling water. Use a blancher, which has a blanching basket and cover. Or fit a wire basket into a large kettle, and add the cover.

For each pound of prepared vegetable use at least 1 gallon of boiling water in the blancher or kettle. Put vegetables in blanching basket or wire basket and lower into the boiling water. A wire cover for the basket can be used to keep the vegetables down in the boiling water.

Put lid on blancher or kettle and start counting time immediately. Keep heat high for time given in directions for vegetable you are freezing. Heat 1 minute longer than the time specified if you live 5,000 feet or more above sea level.

To heat in steam. For broccoli, pumpkin, sweetpotatoes, and winter squash both steaming and boiling are satisfactory methods.

To steam, use a kettle with a tight lid and a rack that holds a steaming basket at least 3 inches above the bottom of the kettle. Put an inch or two of water in the kettle and bring the water to a boil.

Put vegetables in the basket in a single layer so that steam reaches all parts quickly. Cover the kettle and keep heat high. Start counting steaming time as soon as the lid is on. Steam 1 minute longer than the time specified in the directions if you live 5,000 feet or more above sea level.

Other ways to heat. Pumpkin, sweetpotatoes, and winter squash may be heated in a pressure cooker or in the oven before freezing. Mushrooms may be heated in fat in a fry pan. Tomatoes for juice may be simmered.

Cooling

After vegetables are heated they should be cooled quickly and thoroughly to stop the cooking.

To cool vegetables heated in boiling water or steam, plunge the basket of vegetables immediately into a large quantity of cold water—60° F. or below. Change water frequently or use cold running water or iced water. If ice is used, you'll need about 1 pound of ice for each pound of vegetable. It will take about as long to cool the food as it does to heat it. When the vegetable is cool, remove it from the water and drain thoroughly.

To cool vegetables heated in the oven, a pressure cooker, or a fry pan—set pan of food in water and change water to speed cooling.

Dry Pack More Practical

Either dry or brine pack may be used for most vegetables to be frozen. However, the dry pack is recommended for all vegetables because preparation for freezing and serving is easier.

Table of Vegetable Yields

The table will help you figure the amount of frozen food you can get from a given amount of a fresh vegetable. The number of pints of frozen vegetables you get depends on the quality, condition, maturity, and variety—and on the way the vegetable is trimmed and cut.

VEGETABLE	FRESH, AS PURCHASED OR PICKED	FROZEN
Asparagus	1 crate (12 2-lb. bunches) 1 to 1½ lb.	15 to 22 pt. 1 pt.
Beans, lima (in pods)	1 bu. (32 lb.) 2 to 2½ lb.	12 to 16 pt. 1 pt.
Beans, snap, green, and wax	1 bu. (30 lb.) ⅔ to 1 lb.	30 to 45 pt. 1 pt.
Beet greens	15 lb. 1 to 1½ lb.	10 to 15 pt. 1 pt.
Beets (without tops)	1 bu. (52 lb.) 1¼ to 1½ lb.	35 to 42 pt. 1 pt.
Broccoli	1 crate (25 lb.) 1 lb.	24 pt. 1 pt.
Brussels sprouts	4 quart boxes 1 lb.	6 pt. 1 pt.
Carrots (without tops)	1 bu. (50 lb.) 1¼ to 1½ lb.	32 to 40 pt. 1 pt.
Cauliflower	2 medium heads 1⅓ lb.	3 pt. 1 pt.
Chard	1 bu. (12 lb.) 1 to 1½ lb.	8 to 12 pt. 1 pt.
Collards	1 bu. (12 lb.) 1 to 1½ lb.	8 to 12 pt. 1 pt.
Corn, sweet (in husks)	1 bu. (35 lb.) 2 to 2½ lb.	14 to 17 pt. 1 pt.
Kale	1 bu. (18 lb.) 1 to 1½ lb.	12 to 18 pt. 1 pt.
Mustard greens	1 bu. (12 lb.) 1 to 1½ lb.	8 to 12 pt. 1 pt.
Peas	1 bu. (30 lb.) 2 to 2½ lb.	12 to 15 pt. 1 pt.
Peppers, sweet	⅔ lb. (3 peppers)	1 pt.
Pumpkin	3 lb.	2 pt.
Spinach	1 bu. (18 lb.) 1 to 1½ lb.	12 to 18 pt. 1 pt.
Squash, summer	1 bu. (40 lb.) 1 to 1¼ lb.	32 to 40 pt. 1 pt.
Squash, winter	3 lb.	2 pt.
Sweetpotatoes	⅔ lb.	1 pt.

DIRECTIONS FOR VEGETABLES

Asparagus

Select young, tender stalks with compact tips. Sort according to thickness of stalk.

Wash asparagus thoroughly and cut or break off and discard tough parts of stalks. Leave spears in lengths to fit the package or cut in 2-inch lengths.

Heat stalks in boiling water according to thickness of stalk:

Small stalks	2 minutes
Medium stalks	3 minutes
Large stalks	4 minutes

Cool promptly in cold water and drain.

Pack into containers, leaving no head space. When packing spears, alternate tips and stem ends. In containers that are wider at the top than bottom, pack asparagus with tips down. Seal and freeze.

Beans, Lima

Select well-filled pods. Beans should be green but not starchy or mealy. Shell and sort according to size, or leave beans in pods to be shelled after heating and cooling. Heat in boiling water.

Small beans or pods	2 minutes
Medium beans or pods	3 minutes
Large beans or pods	4 minutes

Cool promptly in cold water and drain. Pack into containers, leaving 1/2-inch head space. Seal and freeze.

Beans, Shell, Green

Select pods that are plump, not dry or wrinkled. Shell the beans. Heat in boiling water 1 minute. Cool promptly in cold water and drain. Pack into containers, leaving 1/2-inch head space. Seal and freeze.

Beans, Snap, Green, or Wax

Select young, tender, stringless beans that snap when broken. Wash thoroughly; then remove ends. Cut in 1- or 2-inch pieces, or slice lengthwise into strips for frenched (julienne-style) snap beans. Heat in boiling water for 3 minutes. Chill promptly in cold water and drain. Pack into containers, leaving 1/2-inch head space. Seal and freeze.

Other vegetables may be frozen in much the same way as snap beans. Beans are heated in boiling water before they are frozen—the most satisfactory home method for nearly all vegetables.

Select young, tender, stringless beans that snap when broken. Allow 2/3 to 1 pound of fresh beans for 1 pint frozen. Wash thoroughly. Cut beans into 1- or 2-inch pieces or slice them lengthwise.

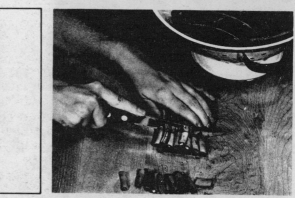

Put beans in blanching basket, lower basket into boiling water, and cover. Heat for 3 minutes. Keep heat high under the water.

Plunge basket of heated beans into cold water to stop the cooking. It takes about as long to cool vegetables as to heat them. When beans are cool, remove them from water and drain.

Leave 1/2-inch head space and seal by twisting and folding back top of bag and tying with a string. Freeze beans at once. Store at 0° F. or below. If the bags used are of materials that become brittle at low temperatures, they need an outside carton for protection.

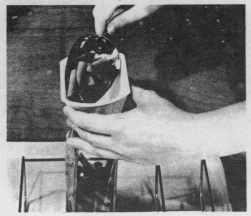

Pack the beans into bags or other containers. A stand to hold the bags makes filling easier. A funnel helps keep the sealing edges clean.

Beans, Soybeans, Green

Select firm, well-filled, bright-green pods. Wash. Heat beans in pods 5 minutes in boiling water, and cool promptly in cold water. Squeeze soybeans out of pods. Pack soybeans into containers, leaving 1/2-inch head space. Seal and freeze.

Beets

Select young or mature beets not more than 3 inches across. Wash and sort according to size. Trim tops, leaving 1/2 inch of stems.

Cook in boiling water until tender—for small beets, 25 to 30 minutes; for medium-size beets, 45 to 50 minutes. Cool promptly in cold water. Peel and cut into slices or cubes. Pack beets into containers, leaving 1/2-inch head space. Seal and freeze.

Broccoli

Select tight, compact, dark-green heads with tender stalks free from woodiness. Wash, peel stalks, and trim. If necessary to remove insects, soak for 1/2 hour in a solution made of 4 teaspoons salt to 1 gallon cold water. Split lengthwise into pieces so that flowerets are not more than 1-1/2 inches across.

Heat in steam 5 minutes or in boiling water 3 minutes. Cool promptly in cold water and drain.

Pack broccoli so some heads are at each end of the container—to get more broccoli in the package. No head space is needed. Press lid on firmly to seal. Freeze at once. Store at 0° F. or below.

Brussels Sprouts

Select green, firm, and compact heads. Examine heads carefully to make sure they are free from insects. Trim, removing coarse outer leaves. Wash thoroughly. Sort into small, medium, and large sizes. Heat in boiling water:

Small heads	3 minutes
Medium heads	4 minutes
Large heads	5 minutes

Cool promptly in cold water and drain. Pack brussels sprouts into containers, leaving no head space. Seal and freeze.

Cabbage or Chinese Cabbage

Frozen cabbage or Chinese cabbage is suitable for use only as a cooked vegetable. Select freshly picked, solid heads. Trim coarse outer leaves from head. Cut into medium to coarse shreds or thin wedges, or separate head into leaves. Heat in boiling water 1-1/2 minutes. Cool promptly in cold water and drain. Pack cabbage into containers, leaving 1/2-inch head space. Seal and freeze.

Carrots

Select tender, mild-flavored carrots. Remove tops, wash, and peel. Leave small carrots whole. Cut others into 1/4-inch cubes, thin slices, or lengthwise strips. Heat in boiling water:

Whole carrots, small	5 minutes
Diced or sliced	2 minutes
Lengthwise strips	2 minutes

Cool promptly in cold water and drain. Pack carrots into containers, leaving 1/2-inch head space. Seal and freeze.

Cauliflower

Choose firm, tender, snow white heads. Break or cut into pieces about 1 inch across. Wash well. If necessary to remove insects, soak for 30 minutes in a solution of salt and water—4 teaspoons salt to each gallon of water. Drain.

Heat in boiling water containing 4 teaspoons salt to a gallon for 3 minutes. Cool promptly in cold water and drain. Pack cauliflower into containers, leaving no head space. Seal and freeze.

Celery

Select crisp, tender stalks, free from coarse strings and pithiness. Wash thoroughly, trim, and cut stalks into 1-inch lengths.

Heat for 3 minutes in boiling water. Cool promptly in cold water and drain. Pack celery into containers, leaving 1/2-inch head space. Seal and freeze.

Corn, Sweet

Whole-kernel and cream-style. Select ears with plump, tender kernels and thin, sweet milk. If the milk is thick and starchy it is better to freeze corn as cream-style.

Husk ears, remove silk, and wash the corn. Heat ears in boiling water for 4 minutes. Cool promptly in cold water and drain.

For whole-kernel corn, cut kernels from cob at about two-thirds the depth of the kernels.

For cream-style corn, cut corn from the cob at about the center of the kernels. Scrape the cobs with the back of the knife to remove the juice and the heart of the kernel.

Pack corn into containers, leaving 1/2-inch head space. Seal and freeze.

On-the-cob. Select same as for whole-kernel sweet corn.

Husk, remove silk, wash, and sort ears according to size. Heat in boiling water:

Small ears (1-1/4 inches or less in diameter	7 minutes
Medium ears (1-1/4 to 1-1/2 inches in diameter):	9 minutes
Large ears (over 1-1/2 inches in diameter	11 minutes

Cool promptly in cold water and drain. Pack ears into containers or wrap in moisture-vapor-resistant material. Seal and freeze.

Greens—Beet Greens, Chard, Collards, Kale, Mustard Greens, Spinach, Turnip Greens

Select young, tender leaves. Wash well. Remove tough stems and imperfect leaves. Cut leaves of chard into pieces as desired. Heat in boiling water for the following periods:

Beet greens, kale, chard, mustard greens, turnip greens:	2 minutes
Collards:	3 minutes
Spinach and New Zealand spinach	2 minutes
Very tender leaves:	1-1/2 minutes

Cool promptly in cold water and drain. Pack greens into containers, leaving 1/2-inch head space. Seal and freeze.

Kohlrabi

Select young, tender, mild-flavored kohlrabi, small to medium in size. Cut off tops and roots. Wash, peel, and leave whole or dice in 1/2-inch cubes. Heat in boiling water:

Whole kohlrabi: 3 minutes
Cubes: 1 minute

Cool promptly in cold water and drain. Pack whole kohlrabi into containers or wrap in moisture-vapor-resistant material. Seal and freeze.

Okra

Select young, tender, green pods. Wash thoroughly. Cut off stems in such a way as not to cut open seed cells. Heat in boiling water.

Small pods   3 minutes
Large pods   4 minutes

Cool promptly in cold water and drain. Leave whole or slice crosswise. Pack into containers, leaving 1/2-inch head space. Seal and freeze.

Parsnips

Choose small to medium-size parsnips that are tender and free from woodiness. Remove tops, wash, peel, and cut in 1/2-inch cubes or slices. Heat in boiling water 2 minutes. Cool promptly in cold water; drain.

Pack into containers, leaving 1/2-inch head space. Seal and freeze.

Peas, Field (Blackeye)

Select well-filled flexible pods with tender seeds. Shell peas, discarding those that are hard.

Heat in boiling water for 2 minutes. Cool promptly in cold water and drain. Pack into containers, leaving 1/2-inch head space. Seal and freeze.

Peas, Green

Choose bright-green, plump, firm pods with sweet, tender peas. Do not use immature or tough peas. Shell peas. Heat in boiling water and drain. Pack peas into containers, leaving 1/2-inch head space. Seal and freeze.

Peppers, Sweet or Hot

Sweet. Peppers frozen without heating are best for use in uncooked foods. Heated peppers are easier to pack and good for use in cooking.

Select firm, crisp, thick-walled peppers. Wash, cut out stems, cut in half, and remove seeds. If desired, cut into 1/2-inch strips or rings. Heat in boiling water if desired:

Halves   3 minutes
Slices   2 minutes

Cool promptly in cold water and drain.

If peppers have not been heated, pack into containers, leaving no head space. Seal and freeze. If peppers have been heated, leave 1/2-inch head space.

Hot. Wash and stem peppers. Pack into small containers, leaving no head space. Seal and freeze.

Pumpkin

Select full-colored, mature pumpkin with texture that is fine rather than coarse and stringy. Wash, cut into quarters or smaller pieces, and remove seeds. Cook pumpkin pieces until soft in boiling water, in steam, in a pressure cooker, or in the oven. Remove pulp from rind and mash it or press it through a sieve. To cool, place pan containing pumpkin in cold water. Stir pumpkin occasionally.

Pack into containers, leaving 1/2-inch head space. Seal and freeze.

Rutabagas

Select young, tender, medium-sized rutabagas with no tough fibers. Cut off tops, wash, and peel.

Cubed. Cut into 1/2-inch cubes. Heat in boiling water for 2 minutes. Cool promptly in cold water; drain. Pack into containers, leaving 1/2-inch head space. Seal and freeze.

Mashed. Cut rutabagas in pieces. Cook until tender in boiling water and drain. Mash or press through a sieve. To cool, place pan containing rutabagas in cold water. Stir rutabagas occasionally. Pack into containers, leaving 1/2-inch head space. Seal and freeze.

Squash, Summer or Winter

Summer. Select young squash with small seeds and tender rind. Wash, cut in 1/2-inch slices. Heat in boiling water for 3 minutes. Cool squash promptly in cold water and drain. Pack into containers, leaving 1/2-inch head space. Seal and freeze.

Winter. Select firm, mature squash. Wash, cut into pieces, and remove seeds. Cook pieces until soft in boiling water, in steam, in a pressure cooker, or in the oven. Remove pulp from rind and mash or press through a sieve. To cool, place pan containing squash in cold water and stir squash occasionally. Pack into containers, leaving 1/2-inch head space. Seal and freeze.

Sweetpotatoes

Sweetpotatoes may be packed whole, sliced, or mashed. Choose medium to large mature sweetpotatoes that have been cured. Sort according to size, and wash.

Cook until almost tender in water, in steam, in a pressure cooker, or in the oven. Let stand at room temperature until cool. Peel sweetpotatoes; cut in halves, slice, or mash.

If desired, to prevent darkening, dip whole sweetpotatoes or slices for 5 seconds in a solution of 1 tablespoon citric acid or 1/2 cup lemon juice to 1 quart water. To keep mashed sweetpotatoes from darkening, mix 2 tablespoons orange or lemon juice with each quart of mashed sweetpotatoes.

Pack into containers, leaving 1/2-inch head space. Seal and freeze.

For variety. Roll cooked sweetpotato slices in sugar. Pack into containers, leaving 1/2-inch head space. Seal and freeze.

Or pack whole or sliced cooked sweetpotatoes in containers, cover with cold syrup (made of equal parts by measure of sugar and water). Leave head space (for liquid pack). Seal and freeze.

Tomatoes

Juice. Wash, sort, and trim firm, vine-ripened tomatoes. Cut in quarters or eighths. Simmer 5 to 10 minutes. Press through a sieve. If desired, season with 1 teaspoon salt to each quart of juice. Pour into containers, leaving head space (for juices). Seal and freeze.

Stewed. Remove stem ends, peel, and quarter ripe tomatoes. Cover and cook until tender (10 to 20 minutes). Place pan containing tomatoes in cold water to cool. Pack into containers, leaving head space (for liquid pack). Seal and freeze.

Turnips

Select small to medium, firm turnips that are tender and have a mild flavor. Wash, peel, and cut into 1/2-inch cubes. Heat in boiling water and drain. Pack into containers, leaving 1/2-inch head space. Seal and freeze.

STORAGE

Fresh, perishable foods should be used soon after harvest or purchase. If storage is necessary, maintain the proper temperature and humidity. Use fresh foods as soon as possible, before they undergo a loss of quality. Even under the best storage conditions, freshness and nutritive value can be lost if foods are stored too long.

Under poor storage conditions, foods held too long often spoil. Some kinds of spoilage are harmful to health; others are not. It is not always possible to distinguish between the two kinds.

Among the signals that indicate dangerous bacterial spoilage are off-odors in foods and a sour taste in bland foods.

Low temperatures are required in the storage of many perishable foods. Low temperatures retard quality losses and delay spoilage by slowing the action of enzymes naturally present, and by slowing the growth of spoilage organisms that may be present.

Storage Needs Vary

Foods vary in the degree of temperature and the amount of moisture needed to retain quality in storage.

Although most fresh, perishable foods keep longest and best in the refrigerator, certain varieties of apples and some root vegetables keep well in a cool basement or outdoor cellar or pit. A few fruits and vegetables can be kept successfully at room temperatures.

Green leafy vegetables keep their crispness and nutrients best in cold, moist air. On the other hand, too much moisture in the air around cherries and berries encourages the growth of mold and rot.

Check the storage facilities you have. Do you have a cool, dark place to store root vegetables? If not, cultivate only small quantities of these vegetables.

Do you have adequate hydrator space in the refrigerator? If not, have plastic bags on hand to store food that must be kept moist. Plastic containers with tight fitting lids are also suitable. Any refrigerated food that may lose quality through drying should be kept covered.

Know the refrigerator you use; locate its coldest spots. Does the refrigerator maintain a uniform temperature? Purchase a reliable thermometer to check refrigerator temperature.

Temperatures in the Refrigerator

The temperature in frostless and self-defrosting refrigerators is fairly uniform throughout the cabinet, including the storage area in the door.

In refrigerators that must be defrosted manually, the coldest area outside the freezing unit is the chill tray located just below it. The area at the bottom of the cabinet is the warmest. The door and hydrator storage areas are usually several degrees higher than the rest of the refrigerator.

When air circulates in the refrigerator, the cooler air moves downward and forces the warmer air near the bottom to rise. This air motion dries out any uncovered or unwrapped food.

In most refrigerators, with the control set for normal operation, the temperature in the general storage area is usually below 40°F. You can check the temperature in your refrigerator by placing a thermometer at different locations in the cabinet. If the temperature is above 40°F., regulate the control to maintain temperatures below 40°F.

Frequent opening of the refrigerator door, especially on warm, humid days, or an accumulation of thick frost on the freezing unit, raises the refrigerator's temperatures.

The freezing compartments of home refrigerators are not designed to give a temperature of 0°F.—the temperature needed for prolonged storage of frozen foods. Hold frozen foods in these compartments only a few days. In refrigerator-freezers where temperature can be maintained at 0°F. in the freezer cabinet, food may be kept for the same storage periods as in a freezer.

Use the refrigerator properly. Do not overcrowd it—allow for air circulation. Defrost when needed.

STORAGE DIRECTIONS

Fruits

Plan to use fresh fruits promptly while they are sound and flavorful. Because fruits are fragile they need special handling to keep them from being crushed or bruised. The softened tissues of bruised and crushed fruits permit the entrance of spoilage organisms that quickly break down quality.

Sort fruits before storing. Bruised or decayed fruit will contaminate sound, firm fruit.

Apples: Store mellow apples uncovered in the refrigerator. Unripe or hard apples are best held at cool room temperature (60°-70°F.) until ready to eat. Use ripe apples within a month.

Apricots, Nectarines, Peaches, and Pears: Allow these fruits to ripen at room temperature, then refrigerate. Use within 3 to 5 days.

Berries and Cherries: Store covered in refrigerator to prevent moisture loss. Do not wash or stem before storing. Use within 2 to 3 days.

Citrus Fruits: These fruits are best stored at a cool room temperature (60°-70°F.). Use within 2 weeks. Citrus fruits may also be stored uncovered in the refrigerator.

Melons: Keep at room temperature until ripe, then refrigerate. When storing cut melon, cover and refrigerate.

Canned Fruit, Canned Fruit Juices: After canned fruits and canned fruit juices have been opened, cover and store them in the refrigerator. They can be safely stored in the original containers. But for better flavor retention, storage in glass or plastic is recommended.

Plums: Plums are generally ripe when picked or sold. Refrigerate and use within 3 to 5 days.

Vegetables

The fresher the vegetable, the better it is when eaten.

With only a few exceptions vegetables keep best in the refrigerator.

The exceptions—potatoes, sweetpotatoes, mature onions, hard-rind squashes, eggplant, and rutabagas—keep well in cool rather than in cold storage.

Sort vegetables before storing them. Use immediately any vegetables that are bruised or soft. Discard any that show evidence of decay.

The vegetable crisper in your refrigerator performs better if it is at least two-thirds full. If crisper is less full than this, vegetables will keep better if they are put in plastic bags before being placed in crisper. Always store vegetables in plastic bags or plastic containers if they are not stored in the crisper.

Asparagus: Do not wash before storing. Store in the refrigerator in crisper, plastic bags, or plastic containers. Use within 2 or 3 days.

Broccoli and Brussels Sprouts: Store in refrigerator in crisper, plastic bags, or plastic containers. Use within 3 to 5 days.

Cabbage, Cauliflower, Celery, and Snap Beans: Store in the refrigerator in crisper, plastic bags, or plastic containers. Use cabbage within 1 or 2 weeks; use cauliflower, celery and snap beans within 1 week.

Carrots, Beets, Parsnips, Radishes, and Turnips: Remove tops. Store in refrigerator in plastic bags or plastic containers. Use within 2 weeks.

Green Peas and Lima Beans: Leave in pods and store in refrigerator. Use within 3 to 5 days.

Lettuce and other Salad Greens: Wash. Drain well. Store in crisper in the refrigerator in plastic bags or plastic containers to reduce loss of moisture. Use within 1 week.

Onions: Store mature onions at room temperature, or slightly cooler, in loosely woven or open-mesh containers. Stored this way, they keep several months. They sprout and decay at high temperature and in high humidity.

Keep green onions cold and moist in the refrigerator. Store in plastic bags. Use within 3 to 5 days.

Peppers and Cucumbers: Wash and dry. Store in crisper or in plastic bags in the refrigerator. Use within 1 week.

Potatoes: Store in a dark, dry place with good ventilation away from any source of heat, with a temperature of about 45° to 50°F. Potatoes stored in this manner will keep for several months. Light causes greening, which lowers eating quality. High temperatures hasten sprouting and shriveling. If stored at room temperature, use within a week.

Rhubarb: This vegetable is often used as a fruit. It is ready to use when harvested. Refrigerate and use within 3 to 5 days.

Spinach, Kale, Collards, Chard, Beets, Turnips, and Mustard Greens: Wash thoroughly in cold water. Lift out of the water as grit settles to the bottom of the pan. Drain well. Store in refrigerator in crisper or in plastic bags. Use within 3 to 5 days.

Squash, Summer Varieties: Store in crisper, plastic bags or containers and use within 3 to 5 days.

Sweet Corn: Store, unhusked and uncovered, in the refrigerator. Use as soon as possible for sweetest flavor.

Sweetpotatoes, Hard-Rind Squashes, Eggplant, and Rutabagas: Store at cool room temperature (around 60°F.). Temperatures below 50°F. may cause chilling injury. These will keep several months at 60°F., but only about a week at room temperature.

Tomatoes: Store ripe tomatoes uncovered in the refrigerator. They can be stored in the refrigerator up to a week depending on ripeness when stored. Keep unripe tomatoes at room temperature away from direct sunlight until they ripen.

EAT'EM UP: RECIPES

Cooking Fresh Vegetables

Preparing

Remove bruised, wilted, yellowed, or tough portions from fresh vegetables. Trim sparingly to avoid excessive loss of food and nutrients. If root vegetables and potatoes are pared before cooking, make parings thin.

Dark-green outer leaves of cabbage, lettuce, and other leafy green vegetables are high in nutrients, so don't discard them unless they are wilted or tough. Remove woody midribs from kale leaves—there is little loss of nutritive value and the kale tastes better.

Wash vegetables thoroughly before cooking. Use plenty of water for leafy greens; lift them from water to let sand and grit settle.

Soak fresh brussels sprouts and broccoli in cold salt water for a short time to remove insects if any are present. Cover potatoes with water to prevent darkening if held after paring. Long soaking of most vegetables, however, is not desirable because some nutrients dissolve in the water.

Boiling

To insure the best flavor, color, texture, and food value in vegetables, cook them only until they are tender. Vegetables cooked whole in skins retain most of their nutritive value. To shorten cooking time—cut, slice, dice, or coarsely shred vegetables.

The amount of water used in cooking is important—the less water, the more nutrients retained in the cooked vegetable.

For young, tender vegetables, ½ to 1 cup of water is usually enough for six servings. Water to cover is needed for some older root vegetables that require longer cooking. Spinach and other greens need only the water clinging to their leaves from washing if cooked over low heat in a pan with a tight-fitting lid. Tomatoes can be cooked in their own juice.

Directions for boiling fresh vegetables:

Bring salted water to a boil (use ½ to 1 teaspoon salt for six servings of vegetable).

Add vegetable. Cover, and quickly bring water back to a boil.

Reduce heat and cook gently until vegetable is just tender.

Serve immediately; flavor and nutritive value may be lost if vegetables are allowed to stand.

Boiling Guide for Fresh Vegetables

Vegetable	Cooking time after water returns to boil	Approximate amount as purchased for six servings (about ½ cup each)
	Minutes	*Pounds*
Asparagus	10 to 20 (whole spears)	2½ for spears.
	5 to 15 (cuts and tips)	1¾ for cuts and tips.
Beans, lima	25 to 30	2¾ in pods.
Beans, snap (green or wax)	12 to 16 (1-inch pieces)	1.
Beets	30 to 45 (young, whole)	} 2½ with tops or
	45 to 90 (older, whole)	} 1½ without tops.
	15 to 25 (sliced or diced)	
Broccoli	10 to 15 (heavy stalk split)	2.
Brussels sprouts	15 to 20	1½.
Cabbage	3 to 10 (shredded)	1¼.
	10 to 15 (wedges)	1½.
Carrots	15 to 20 (young, whole)	
	20 to 30 (older, whole)	} 1½ without tops.
	10 to 20 (sliced or diced)	
Cauliflower	8 to 15 (separated)	} 2.
	15 to 25 (whole)	
Celery	15 to 18 (cut-up)	1½.
Corn	5 to 15 (on cob)	3 in husks.
Kale	10 to 15	1¼ untrimmed.
Okra	10 to 15	1¼.
Onions, mature	15 to 30	1¾.
Parsnips	20 to 40 (whole)	} 1½.
	8 to 15 (quartered)	
Peas	12 to 16	3 in pods.
Potatoes	25 to 40 (whole, medium)	} 1½.
	20 to 25 (quartered)	
	10 to 15 (diced)	1¼.
Spinach	3 to 10	1½ prepackaged.
Squash, summer	8 to 15 (sliced)	1½.
Squash, winter	15 to 20 (cut-up)	2½.
Sweetpotatoes	35 to 55 (whole)	2.
Tomatoes	7 to 15 (cut-up)	1¼.
Turnip greens	10 to 30	2¾ prepackaged.
Turnips	20 to 30 (whole)	} 1¾ without tops.
	10 to 20 (cut-up)	

Pressure Cooking

In cooking vegetables, follow the directions that came with your cooker, but learn to adjust cooking time to suit the quality of the vegetable being cooked. Very young, tender vegetables may require a shorter cooking time than is recommended. Even 1 or 2 minutes extra cooking can cause undesirable color, changes in texture, and loss of nutrients.

Directions for pressure cooking:

Bring pressure up quickly.
Time the cooking period exactly.
Reduce pressure as quickly as possible when time is up.
Season vegetables in the same ways as plain boiled vegetables.

French Frying

Vegetables that can be french fried successfully include potatoes; sweetpotatoes; breaded green pepper rings; batter dipped eggplant sticks; parsnips and onion rings. Before frying potatoes or sweetpotatoes, rinse them quickly in cold water to remove surface starch.

Dry thoroughly.

Do not overload the fry basket when french frying. If too much food is put into the basket at one time, the temperature of the fat drops excessively, cooking slows down, and the vegetables absorb more fat.

Fill kettle one-third full of fat or oil and heat to 370°-385° F. Have fry basket in fat.

Raise basket and add enough vegetable to cover bottom of basket.

Lower basket gently into fat. If fat bubbles much, lift and lower basket several times until bubbling subsides.

Fry until vegetable is cooked through and golden brown.

Lift basket from fat. Drain a few seconds; then pour vegetable onto absorbent paper.

Season. Spread fried vegetable on cookie sheet and place in warm oven to keep warm while frying additional vegetables.

Panning

Panning is cooking shredded or sliced vegetables in a small amount of fat and water on top of the range and is a good way to prepare snap beans, cabbage, carrots, corn, spinach, and summer squash.

Directions for panning:

Shred or slice vegetable.

Heat in fat (butter, margarine or drippings) in heavy frypan over moderate heat.

Add vegetable and sprinkle with salt.

Add water and cover pan to hold in steam.

Cook over low heat until vegetable is tender; stir occasionally to prevent sticking.

Cooking Frozen Vegetables

Frozen vegetables may be prepared by boiling in a small amount of water, or you can cook them in a moderate oven while you are baking other foods. Cooked frozen vegetables are seasoned and served like fresh vegetables. If you like you can cream or scallop them or add them to souffles, soups, or salads.

Boiling

Thawing before cooking is not necessary for most frozen vegetables. Leafy vegetables, however, cook more evenly if thawed just enough to separate the leaves before you put them in boiling water. It is a good idea to partially thaw corn-on-the-cob before cooking it so that the cob will be heated through by the time the corn is cooked.

Guide for Cooking Panned Vegetables
6 servings (½ cup each)

Vegetable	Amount of—				Cooking time
	Vegetable	Fat	Salt	Water	
	Quarts	*Tablespoons*	*Teaspoons*		*Minutes*
Beans, snap, (green or wax) sliced in 1-inch pieces	1	1½	½	⅔ cup	20 to 25.
Cabbage, finely shredded	1½	1½	¾	3 tablespoons	6 to 8.
Carrots, thinly sliced	1	2	½	3 tablespoons	10.
Corn, cut	1	1½	½	⅓ cup	15 to 18.
Spinach, finely shredded	3	2	½	--------------	6 to 8.
Summer squash, thinly sliced	1	1½	½	3 tablespoons	12 to 15.

Cook home frozen vegetables as follows:

Bring lightly salted water to a boil in a covered saucepan. The amount of water varies with the kind of vegetable and the size of the package. For most vegetables, ½-cup of water is enough for a pint package. Use 1-cup water for a pint of lima beans; water to cover for corn-on-the-cob.

Put frozen vegetable into boiling water, cover pan, and bring quickly back to a boil. To insure uniform cooking, it may be necessary to separate pieces with a fork.

When water returns to boiling, reduce heat and start to count time.

Since some vitamins and minerals are in the cooking liquid, serve the cooking liquid with the vegetable whenever practicable, or use it in sauces, soups, or gravies.

Heat home-canned vegetables the same way if you are sure they have been processed correctly at the recommended temperature. If you are not absolutely sure, bring vegetables to a rolling boil in the liquid, then cover and boil for at least 10 minutes. Boil spinach and corn 20 minutes. Don't use food that shows any sign of spoilage such as foaming or off-odor during heating.

Boiling Guide for Frozen Vegetables		
Vegetable	Cooking time after water returns to boil	Approximate amount as purchased for six servings (½ cup each)
	Minutes	*Ounces*
Asparagus, whole	5 to 10	24
Beans, lima	10 to 18	18
Beans, snap (green or wax), cut	12 to 20	16
Broccoli spears	8 to 15	22
Brussels sprouts	10 to 15	20
Carrots, sliced or diced	5 to 10	18
Cauliflower	5 to 8	20
Corn:		
Whole kernel	3 to 6	20
On cob	3 to 5	32
Kale	8 to 12	25
Peas	3 to 5	18
Potatoes, small, whole	10 to 12	21
Spinach	5 to 14	25
Squash, summer, sliced	10 to 12	22
Turnip greens	15 to 20	27

Baking

Partly defrost vegetables to separate the pieces. Spread vegetables in a greased casserole, add seasonings as desired, and cover. Bake until just tender.

At 350° F. (moderate oven) most vegetables require approximately 45 minutes. Cooking time varies with the size of pieces and how much they were thawed before baking.

Heating Canned Vegetables

Commercially canned vegetables need reheating only. Cook gently until just heated through.

SEASONING WITH HERBS AND SPICES

Spices and herbs can add that special touch to vegetable dishes. However, they must be used sparingly or they overpower, rather than enhance, the natural flavor of vegetables. One-fourth to ½ teaspoon of most dried herbs and spices is enough for 2 cups of vegetables.

The term "spices," as generally used, includes the herbs as well as true spices. Herbs are leaves and sometimes flowers of aromatic plants grown in the Temperate Zone; spices come from the aromatic plants grown in the Tropics.

Dried herbs are more concentrated than fresh

herbs. Use about ¼ teaspoon of a dried herb for 2 cups of vegetables and add it at the beginning of the cooking period. With fresh herbs, increase to about ¾ to 1 teaspoon for 2 cups of vegetable. Chop herbs very fine to allow some of the flavoring oils to escape. Heat chopped herbs in melted butter and add to vegetable after it has been cooked.

SPICES AND HERBS

Vegetable	Spice or herb
Asparagus	Mustard seed, sesame seed, or tarragon.
Beans, lima	Marjoram, oregano, sage, savory, tarragon, or thyme.
Beans, snap	Basil, dill, marjoram, mint, mustard seed, oregano, savory, tarragon, or thyme.
Beets	Allspice, bay leaves, caraway seed, cloves, dill, ginger, mustard seed, savory, or thyme.
Broccoli	Caraway seed, dill, mustard seed, or tarragon.
Brussels sprouts	Basil, caraway seed, dill, mustard seed, sage, or thyme.
Cabbage	Caraway seed, celery seed, dill, mint, mustard seed, nutmeg, savory, or tarragon.
Carrots	Allspice, bay leaves, caraway seed, dill, fennel, ginger, mace, marjoram, mint, nutmeg, or thyme.
Cauliflower	Caraway seed, celery salt, dill, mace, or tarragon.
Cucumbers	Basil, dill, mint, or tarragon.
Eggplant	Marjoram or oregano.
Onions	Caraway seed, mustard seed, nutmeg, oregano, sage, or thyme.
Peas	Basil, dill, marjoram, mint, oregano, poppy seed, rosemary, sage, or savory.
Potatoes	Basil, bay leaves, caraway seed, celery seed, dill, chives, mustard seed, oregano, poppy seed, or thyme.
Salad greens	Basil, chives, dill, or tarragon.
Spinach	Basil, mace, marjoram, nutmeg, or oregano.
Squash	Allspice, basil, cinnamon, cloves, fennel, ginger, mustard seed, nutmeg, or rosemary.
Sweetpotatoes	Allspice, cardamom, cinnamon, cloves, or nutmeg.
Tomatoes	Basil, bay leaves, celery seed, oregano, sage, sesame seed, tarragon, or thyme.

EAT 'EM UP: RECIPES

Garden Relish

½ teaspoon salt
½ teaspoon Tabasco
2 teaspoons sugar
½ cup white vinegar
2 tablespoons water
2 teaspoons soy sauce
2 cups sliced radishes
½ cup sliced scallions

Make marinade by combining salt, Tabasco, sugar, vinegar, water and soy sauce in small bowl. Add sliced radishes and scallions; refrigerate at least 2 hours, turning occasionally. Makes 2½ cups.

Lima Bean Creole

20 oz. frozen lima beans
6 slices bacon
¼ cup finely chopped onion
2 tablespoons chopped green pepper
½ teaspoon salt
Pepper, as desired
2 cups cooked or canned tomatoes

Cook beans; drain. Fry bacon; drain on absorbent paper. In 2 tablespoons bacon drippings, brown onion and green pepper. Crumble bacon. Add browned onion and green pepper, bacon, seasonings, and tomatoes to beans. Cover and simmer gently 15 minutes. Makes 6 servings.
OR
Green bean creole: Use 20. oz. frozen green beans instead of lima beans.
OR
Eggplant creole: Use 1 medium-size eggplant, pared and cubed, instead of beans. Do not cook eggplant before combining with other ingredients. Increase salt to 1 teaspoon. Cook 15 to 25 minutes, until eggplant is tender.

Braised Lettuce with Carrots

4 small heads of lettuce (or equivalent)
Water to cover
1 teaspoon salt
2 tablespoons finely chopped onion
2 tablespoons finely chopped parsley
4 tablespoons finely chopped carrots
1 cup beef bouillon, double strength
Paprika

Place washed lettuce in saucepan and pour in enough boiling water to cover, stirring in salt. Cover pan and simmer for 1 to 2 minutes. Drain thoroughly in colander. Cut heads in half and place in skillet, cut sides down. Mix onion, parsley, and carrots with beef broth and add to lettuce. Cover and simmer over low heat for 10 minutes. Place in serving bowl, pour the remaining liquid over lettuce, sprinkle lightly with paprika, if desired, and serve. Makes 4 servings.

Creamed Peas and Mushrooms

2 (4-oz.) cans mushrooms
1 quart fresh peas, cooked
1 tablespoon butter
Salt and pepper
1 tablespoon flour
1 cup cream
1 egg yolk

Make a cream sauce by melting the butter, stir in flour and seasoning gradually, making a smooth paste. Add the mushrooms and peas just before serving and blend in thoroughly the beaten yolk of one egg. Serve on triangles of toast.

Rutabaga Strips

1-1½ cups rutabaga, cut in ¼-inch strips
1 tablespoon butter or margarine
½ cup water
1 chicken bouillon cube
1 tablespoon sugar

Combine all ingredients in a saucepan. Cook covered until rutabaga is tender, about 15 minutes. Makes 2 servings.

Baked Potatoes or Sweetpotatoes

1 potato per serving

Wash and dry vegetables. Rub with a little fat to soften skin. Prick with a fork to allow steam to escape during baking and to prevent bursting. Bake at 425° F. (hot oven) until tender—for medium-size potatoes, 50-60 minutes; for sweetpotatoes, 35-60 minutes.

If other foods are to be cooked at 350° F. or 375° F. (moderate oven), potatoes or sweetpotatoes may be baked along with them. Allow 10 to 20 minutes longer than times given above.
OR:

Remove baked potato from skin, mash with butter or margarine and milk, stuff back into skin, and sprinkle with grated cheese or spread with sour cream and chopped chives. Return to oven for 10 minutes or until lightly browned.

Scoop baked sweetpotato from the skin; mash with butter or margarine and milk. Or use 1 tablespoon peanut butter for each sweetpotato in place of butter or margarine, or orange juice and a little grated orange rind in place of the milk. Stuff sweetpotato mixture back into skins and return to oven for 10 minutes.

Baked Onions

2 pounds medium-size onions
1 cup buttered bread cubes
Salt and pepper

Preheat oven to 375° F. (moderate oven). Grease a 1½-quart casserole. Peel onions; cut in half crosswise. Arrange with cut side up in casserole.

Add just enough water to cover bottom of casserole. Sprinkle with salt and pepper. Cover.

Bake 30 minutes. Top with the buttered bread cubes and bake uncovered 15 to 20 minutes longer until cubes are brown and onions are tender. Makes 6 servings.

Dilly Carrots and Beans

¾ cup water
1 teaspoon sugar
½ teaspoon salt
½ teaspoon dill seed
½ pound fresh green snap beans
4 medium carrots
¼ cup Italian dressing

Combine water, sugar, salt, and dill seed in a saucepan; bring to boiling.

Wash and trim green beans; leave whole. Add to boiling water. Simmer 5 minutes.

Cut carrots into thin strips, 2 to 3 inches long. Add to green beans. Boil until both vegetables are tender and liquid is almost evaporated—about 10 minutes.

Add Italian dressing and toss to mix well.

Serve hot, or chill and use in tossed vegetable salads. Makes six ½-cup servings.

Orange-Honeyed Acorn Squash

3 small acorn squash
2 tablespoons frozen orange juice concentrate
¼ cup honey
1 teaspoon salt
2 tablespoons butter or margarine
1/8 teaspoon nutmeg

Preheat oven to 400° F. (hot oven).

Cut squash in half. Remove seeds. Place squash halves in a shallow baking pan.

Combine orange juice concentrate, honey, and salt. Mix well. Put some of the mixture into each squash cavity.

Add 1 teaspoon fat to each squash half. Sprinkle with nutmeg.

Cover pan tightly with aluminum foil to keep steam in and speed cooking. Bake 30 minutes.

Remove foil and continue baking 30 minutes more, or until squash is tender.

Vegetable Medley

2 cups diced turnips
1 cup sliced or diced carrots
½ cup water

½ teaspoon salt
1 cup fresh green peas
2 tablespoons butter or margarine
½ teaspoon salt
1/8 teaspoon pepper

Cook turnips and carrots for 10 minutes in boiling water with ½ teaspoon salt added. Add peas and cook until they are tender, about 5 to 7 minutes. Drain. Season with butter or margarine. Note: Frozen peas can be used in place of fresh peas. Add loose frozen peas when the other vegetables are nearly tender and cook only until peas are tender. Makes six ½-cup servings.

Eggplant-Tomato Casserole

1 large onion, chopped
2 small eggplants, peeled and diced
¼ cup butter or margarine
28 oz. canned tomatoes
1 teaspoon salt
1/8 teaspoon pepper
¼ cup cornflake crumbs

Preheat oven to 350° F. (moderate oven). Cook onion and eggplant in fat until golden brown. Add tomatoes, salt, and pepper. Mix thoroughly. Pour into casserole and top with the crumbs. Bake 30 minutes. Makes six ¾-cup servings.

Summer Squash Bake

1 quart summer squash, sliced
½ cup water
1 teaspoon salt
1 cup medium white sauce
2 beaten eggs
½ cup Cheddar cheese, shredded
½ cup breadcrumbs

Preheat oven to 350° F. (moderate oven). Grease a 1½-quart casserole.
Cook squash in boiling, salted water for 5 minutes. Drain and use vegetable liquid to make the white sauce. Mix squash with white sauce and eggs. Place mixture in casserole. Sprinkle with cheese and breadcrumbs. Bake for 25 minutes. Makes six 2/3-cup servings.

Wilted Spinach

3 slices bacon, cut in ½-inch pieces
2 tablespoons flour
1 tablespoon sugar
1 teaspoon salt
2 tablespoons bacon drippings
¾ cup water
¼ cup vinegar
1 quart raw spinach, coarsely chopped

Fry bacon pieces until crisp. Drain bacon and save drippings. Blend flour, sugar, salt and 2 tablespoons bacon drippings. Stir in water and vinegar and cook until thickened, stirring constantly. Pour hot dressing over spinach. Add bacon. Toss to mix. Makes six 2/3-cup servings.

Cabbage Cooked in Milk

1 quart shredded cabbage
1½ cups milk
2 tablespoons flour
2 tablespoons melted fat
1 teaspoon salt
Dash of pepper

Add cabbage to milk and simmer for 2 minutes. Mix the flour and fat and add a little of the hot milk. Stir into cabbage and cook for 3 or 4 minutes until thickened, stirring constantly. Season with salt and pepper. Makes six ½-cup servings.

Chinese-Style Cauliflower

1 head cauliflower florets, thinly sliced
1 teaspoon salt
1/3 cup hot water
2 tablespoons butter or margarine
2 tablespoons cream
Chives or parsley

Place cauliflower in heavy pan, sprinkle with salt, and add hot water. Cook covered about 5 minutes or until slightly crisp. Add fat and cream. Heat for 1 or 2 minutes longer. Garnish with cut-up chives or parsley. Makes six 1/3-cup servings.

Asparagus Parisienne

2 pounds fresh asparagus
Salted water
¼ pound grated Parmesan
1 pint sour cream
Pepper or cayenne
2 tablespoons bread crumbs
½ stick butter
Paprika

Clean, boil, drain asparagus. Place a layer of asparagus on the bottom of a buttered baking dish. Sprinkle with cheese. Add another layer of vegetable and cheese, etc. Season the sour cream with pepper or cayenne pepper and pour over the asparagus and cheese layers. Sprinkle with bread crumbs, dot with butter, sprinkle with paprika. Bake at 375° for 30 minutes. Makes 6-8 servings.

Carrot-Raisin Relish

8 cups coarsely shredded carrots
1 (15-oz.) package golden raisins
4 cups water
1 cup cider vinegar
1 teaspoon mace
2 cups sugar

In a large saucepan, combine carrots, raisins, water, vinegar and mace. Simmer, covered, 30 minutes. Stir in sugar to dissolve. Cover, simmer 30 minutes longer. Stir frequently. Pour relish into 6 (8-oz.) hot, sterilized preserving jars. Seal with melted paraffin or cap according to manufacturer's directions; or cool and store, covered, in refrigerator. Use as a relish with ham, tongue or poultry. Makes 1-1½ quarts.

Fried Eggplant and Tomato

½ small eggplant
¼ cup flour
½ teaspoon salt
¼ teaspoon oregano
1 small tomato
2 tablespoons (or as needed bacon drippings or other fat
½ teaspoon parsley, chopped

Cut ends from eggplant; cut eggplant into three slices. Remove peel. Mix flour, salt and oregano. Dip eggplant slices into flour mixture. Cut tomato into three slices. Dip in flour mixture. Place fat in frypan. Lightly brown eggplant slices about 2 minutes on each side. Fry tomato slices 1 minute on each side.

To serve, place tomato slices on eggplant and garnish with chopped parsley. Makes 3 servings.

Chinese Celery

2 bunches fresh celery
2 bouillon cubes, chicken or beef
¼ cup water
¼ cup soy sauce
1 sprig parsley, chopped
¼ cup water chestnuts, drained, sliced

Wash and trim celery, removing leaves. Cut rib stalks into ½-inch pieces. Bring water to boil in saucepan, stir in bouillon cubes until dissolved. Add celery, water chestnuts, and chopped parsley. Saute gently, stirring occasionally, until celery is cooked to your taste, preferably fairly crunchy. Serve hot. Makes 6 servings.